T0194141

The Recluse and Other Mystics

The poems of Joshua victor

JOSHUA VICTOR

Order this book online at www.trafford.com
or email orders@trafford.com

Most Trafford titles are also available at major online book retailers.

Print information available on the last page.

ISBN: 978-1-4907-5993-7 (sc)
ISBN: 978-1-4907-5992-0 (hc)
ISBN: 978-1-4907-6005-6 (e)

Library of Congress Control Number: 2015907621

Trafford rev. 08/12/2015

www.trafford.com
North America & international
toll-free: 1 888 232 4444 (USA & Canada)
fax: 812 355 4082

Contents

Book II
Other mystics

Looking at Her

Hey woman
Am I the transparent phantom?
Two obvious black spheres, amber beddings,
Louder than a thousand drunk voices, piercing, the outline of your body expression,
Body language is it too much for me to bear

So my presence will fade into the darkness of today
Until the docile whisper starts to shout-
Black spheres don't let me down
-continue

Please driver slow your speed
Until my senseless eternity, starts with the vast beginning
Of Pandora's Box of great emotion, soaks in the spirit of vulnerability
…your spheres hesitates, no sturdy foundation, boldness,
Frozen and desolate…innocence

That naive suggestion, murders the lustful soul
But my cylindrical spheres doesn't let me down
It is your thin vines, formless and liberal
That found its home with your fingers
Rosy cheeks
Feminine
Breath
Grunts
Sighs of ecstasy
Original ambition on each breath
Tired you say, but I notice my black spheres doesn't let me down

Hips, gifts from the eternal conscience
Sensual but not sexual…
I am grieved…because
I fade, I am nothing
Who am I? A stranger…

Reclined in a stalkers position
Intimidating my body language…
(Foreshadows no interest)

Look up to these spheres!
Woman!
I am overwhelmed by your gallant posture
My soul needs closure…
"I am not intimidating"
I'm just vulnerable
Nervous
Silent because interest haven't been physical
Woman, Damn!
My spheres can't talk
Please…don't ignore me any longer

He will be let out (Ecstasy)

He will be let out…
Out his cage, he will no longer be the indigenous
To be held captive
To be teased
Now he crushed those chains and his talons will grip your neck
-with his rough exterior

Your neck was an ideal at first
La Comida…
A senseless Spanish dinner he wanted
But a supper mother couldn't prepare
But a brutal feast

…soft
Delicate
Pure
With fiery intensity
And pandemonium vision…

He will be let out and he'll sink his talons
Inside your neck and suck out the life from your veins,
Blood streams will meet a boulder
-but you won't bleed!
A vampire…no that's immature
He'll suck until…
You whimper
Softly
Relentlessly
But…cheerfully

An advancing grimace, his eyes will drip fire
His breath will not be caught
-Paws...
Will touch every sensitive canal
Bending your body
Submit now!

Because it's time for him to get out
His hand will gesture...
You will respond
Flinching, but gracefully
Fluently
Your body will adapt as he grow stronger...

You grow weaker
But strong in endurance,
Fatality!
Water, rushing out your canals
Fiercely without ceasing

Your body will ache and grow tired
But pores of your skin will gloss,

Come streams of humid moisture
Body odors
Means...longevity
And hard pressure

You will move, like crystal rolling on the ground
Flexibility
Adaptability
Your hair will not be well
Your head...will ache with blood

-Are you dizzy?
Hold his back for support

Or else you will faint, in the atmosphere of ecstasy
…hellacious pleasure (oh my)
What realms has he taken you to now?
Breathing
Lips dry
But wet
You need water since it has been taken out of you

Tired with endurance
Agony and painful blossoms…

Your fingers turn into talons!
You…to have became a beast
You are flirty…with anger
But you are not frustrated

He tosses you about, like effort with no force
It's simple, you're docile
Because he has been held captive
And all his frustration will pour out…
Inside you!
So hold on…

Now you can't bare it anymore
Your canals invaded
Your body tired
What a mess
Sticky sleet from what clouds…

Tosses you to the ground
Ancestral blessings
Inside!
You're tired
You faint
You're aching
But you're a beast as well so…
You smile

Silent Denise

Sober expression
Haunting silence that corrodes my ears
Eyes center at fiascos
-temporary entertainment

A king without his beautiful courtesans
No girls to entertain him tonight
No wine to quiet his noisy head,
No rest…

A time at night with two pillows on his bed
His silent mistress?
His lover is his garments
Treasures that can never be found
…fate has no mercy

Maybe…because it never gets intimate…
So it makes a man go mad
Nobody to hear his plead
Nobody to hug him

Because a intimate future just cease to exist
…walking the streets
Flaunting his gestures…
It never gets noticed…
By…a woman…
Who feels the same way

A Walk

Cradle me in your arms
-wind
Take me naked in your bosoms
I need warmth…because I constantly find myself in seclusion

Me? I wear dull clothes,
A Nigerian boy
The sun embellishes my eyes
So look at them and fantasize
Dream and celestial
I am benign with my sway

But ill toughen my frown
To hinder you and lose your memory

Oh sun! Shine on me and meditate on my neck
And give it something to cherish,
Just send me…
On my way

Stagger to get in the house
Panting, like a dog
How can I resist…
The frigid liquid…
So sweet…
That goes down my throat
Just thirsty from the walk

Joshua Victor

The Coming of Spring

Wake up!
Friends!
You should not be sleep no more

Your rest
Dormant
Bored
Because of winter romances…

But it's your turn
I call upon the sun
Now arise
Upright
Stretch out
Resurrection…

Stand with color
That foretells pandemonium endeavors

Green in the greenest of creases
Yellow!
Red!
Mahogany!
Maroon, velvet, blue

Your neck green
Perfect by ambitious streams
You were asleep
But now you stretch and sprout out

……oooohhh
What a smell….
I smell…
The coming…of spring

Stranger

Random, Texas winter, blue night,
Unexpected chills,
Wind of bliss
O bliss of silent whispers

Rocks underneath my foot I kick,
Low rumblings, minute
The whisper shines its light on me

Dog!
Position to attack protecting a boring building
Gatekeeper, charge!
-it stops, cease your attack
Because it doesn't smell the fear

Stranger in a foreign land
What type of sprite are you?

Dark, vacant streets, rural,
Antique vintage stores,
-the smell of the elders
Grandfathers, Grandmothers
Hey Dolly!

Pale faces looks at me
Looking…looking at me with big eyes
Frantic, maybe if I draw close
Walking…

I pay close attention,
In a daze of utter scrutiny
My eyes moving around side to side
Comfortable, relaxed paranoia

Joshua Victor

What is that?
Who goes there?
What's behind me?
What did I hear...

They look at me
Oh man I'm in a daze in this foreign land!
No place for me
Because I'm a stranger

Moving, I'm hypnotize by
Silent beauties
Is there something mystic in the air

Do I belong here?
Oh blue nights
Celestial, heavenly skies
Oh stars why can't you tell them
Your child's here

Why do they look down in fear?

Welcome, hey I utter greetings
-quick responses
Move out the way...

Crackling rocks, annoying branches
Tripped, almost falling
Because I'm getting familiar

(Wow) vehicles...
They look at me, passing,
Mouths moving...

What did they say...?
Almost home
A place where I'm known
No gatekeepers at my house

No surprises
My heart grows cool,
It senses familiar warmth…

To hell with trivial pondering
Just a temporary state…

To keep me focused
And not sedated

By scrutinizing…scrutinizing

See

I can see what you think
By the expression that you yield
I can see how you feel your eyes tell it all
Red eyes…you're tired
Grey eyes…hereditary
Yellow eyes…addiction
White eyes, big…excitement
…Take off those shades and quit hiding
Deal with it and scream…

I can tell you more…
But my eyes are yellow because…

I'm a Fiend

Appearance

Feet pressed along, brown dusty vacant roads
Eyes slightly dim, almost closed
Sensitive salt water pours out, like…
Everlasting springs and silent waters

-Why
Because the fingers of the winds
Has reached in and touched my soul

-Nature
You understand me
Grey jacket, collar, take hold of my neck
My hands brown, stained with ash
In my pockets
-so, you don't pay attention to my sway!

Exuberance, joy fills the empty
Vacant body

I need strength, I'm weak

Glasses, spectacles
Bohemian, my eyes stare
And tear into your panes…
Your chandeliers, I know what I'm looking at

…it's you and I see a cold frigid girl
Whimpering at grey windows,

Peaks of sunlight hit my back
Now, I beg for attention…
So what literature would you bring…?
Approach me

…would our souls intertwine?
Hmm
Or a phantasy…
Or intimidation

Solitude is no longer my house
I'll be a child running away…

Sun, stay up,
Eternal day
Night!
Fall asleep

No companion…but
No whimpering
-repeat

The creek

I sat on a hill
In its slumber
The dead grass occupied my bottom
A bag
That was all I brought

The dogs were barking,
Almost with a tune,
Worshipping the coming of spring

By the creek, I sat

Across from me were oblivious houses,
Have their owners forgotten where they were
By myself again
Transient sun, beautiful on Sundays
Grace!

Find favor on me today
The wind blew on me, but it wasn't noisy
Silent in tone, but ostentatious they were
This is only the beginning for a poet

Who walked further today,
The water in the creek was brown
Not for sea animals
But perfect for the escaping muse

Water in my eyes from the winds that invade my pupils
That didn't knock to get in (nature and its arrogance)
Crickets on the ground singing songs as they hide
In the dirt, alerting others, that a giant stranger
Has taken siege on the rooftop of their dirt homes

...but never shall I threaten the indigenous that praises
Voices, I hear, scattered and far away
Faint with joy,
Echoing gaiety across the air

I have sunken into a stupor and...
The birds know I'm a soft recluse
But their eyes take care of me
Their stare protects my heart

...and I'll blow kisses in silence
...to whomever...
Joins me in my utopia

Our Place

Our place,
Will be eccentric,
No place for a common man

The beast will be gentle in disposition
Its fangs will warn off intruders

Our place
Will be embellished,
With quiet terrors
Beautiful storms
Of Venus and Valencia

Enter through the pink door…
Occupied by gargoyles as gatekeepers

Our pleasure,
Romantic,
Secluded, naive "recluses"
Private, sensitive frustration

Our pleasure,
Will be eternal
It'll turn painful

Green hills, with sand…
By repetitive silent tides that seem to be medicine
For a sick mind

The bridge will be a walk through our place
Creatures will come out
Of the sea and show their fins
Of the ancient monarch that was defeated

The sun will shine on the river,
Agile mirrors, will display our biographies
Fish will echo our passions

And we will laugh at the horse that'll…

Never stop running

Calm

Reclined on my brown chest drawer
Blinds cracked, rays of sun sneak in my room
Reclined by the windows
My soul is quiet my head empty with peace…

Flooding
Comfortably quiet
My heart is not at war
Solace!

Who knows would something boisterous happen next
Tranquil I look
Back resting on bedroom furniture
Eyes dim

Notebook in hand, trying to make noise with my expression
Calm like a bohemian sea
Occupied by trees overhanging
Causing dancing shadows to decorate

The surface of peaceful water
Like that
My quiet ecstasy
Like a child is quiet on the swing set

He just learned how to swing
By his self

So he no longer shouts for joy
Because he's gotten use to knowing how to swing

So he's calm swinging
Nuts and bolts squeaking

Like that calm bird
Wandering on the seashore
Looking for quick food
Right before it takes flight

To go to a place where me and you can't go

Calm
Like that, I sit
I'll let the sun radiate the brown that's in my eyes

And let my heart beat
And my legs stretched out
And my head hang low just wondering…
Is this temporary or eternal

The question

I asked myself
One question
(Is there a need for the answer to be ambiguous?)
…when does the poet lose hope?

Some will answer everyday…

But the dawn fills the cavity
To the oblivious exodus
Your exile is temporary
Your solitude is permanent
But one must adapt to pain and ecstasy

Here's the other answer
The muse is hope, the center of life
The colorful lizard that runs madly
…when the rock is lifted

Pushing his life to the edge of the mile high sierras
He dwells within the expressions of the faces
Of the wildlife and other creatures
And screams…

Attack, beat me up
Toss me to the ground
So I can rise up and kill the cubs of Brutus

Joshua Victor

The last answer
To hell with hope
We will stumble on deserted paths everyday
Our mouths, will be dried and lips cracked

Bleeding and we'll constantly thirst
Like the sage in the desert
We will murder to get to an oasis
No hope for a poet it's a search

Wilderness

In the wilderness,
Brown and tan branches
Roots grow deep in the moist ground
The thick mud will surround the ankles if you walk through

No human is allowed
No mobility
No trainers
No tour guides
No experts
No daddy

The trees are tall
Wooden stilts slouched over to make fierce arcs on the right and left
Insect repellants doesn't work
On orange and black six inch winged
Serpents flying faster than air

Noxious to the soul
Noxious to the heart

You're not settled
You walk through hesitantly
The insects with bright colors
Screaming…

Freedom to sting
With porcelain horns ready to defend
And the buzzing is bass for your ears
What a sound of torment

Your eyes bugged
Your heart racing

Joshua Victor

Instruments
Inside

Screaming wild harmony
Suggestive timid tunes
Humid air

Thick like a blanket of white
Heavy on your head
Like wool in heat
Choking your throat

Anaconda reign
The azure has blackened

The noises are ere
Too many to decipher
Frozen in fear
But you keep moving

Strings of sound has made you alert
Your black pupils
Has dilated
To the size of black marbles

Rolling around on a fixed pivot

The wilderness breathes
As you trample through its vertebrae
The animals,
Mystic creatures
looks at you with the death stare

You are the stranger
Their eyes grow yellow…
The call to other creatures
Alerting them!

The lioness roars,
Her fangs sharpened by ambitious fury
You ignore it because…

Her breath smells like regurgitated swamp
That makes perfume on your clothes
You're trembling,
You're weak

While these creatures
Eye you down…

The baboon
Position his mouth
Laughing hysterically
While swinging on the trees

Comedy of violence!
Dark night
Wailing moon
After dusk before dawn

The animals direct you
To the path of human fossils
Skeletons
Have dance their way into the stomach

Of the creatures

But you ignore…

Joshua Victor

One must be scared senseless
A fear that is so riveting
The humid dew
Have blended in with the sweat
That pours through your fleshly sierras

And your armpits
Stained with scared musk
Moisture forbidden
Pain excrete down your ribs

And the bites of the bugs
Have not kicked in

Oh my

Suddenly
You feel claws
Sinking into your neck
And thrust you to the right

And you're on a green moor
Open land by yourself

You're weak…
Sleep o child

Wake up

Its morning
You survived

Comedy of Scrutiny

Ah
Here I am
Suspended inside this circular vortex
Riveting
A daze
Hanging by gentle wings

The windows to outside

Displays
Marvelous
Colors
Breathing

A vibrant show
Green and milky, white
Yellow, rays, and orange

Fluorescent plants absorb
Pale, bruised sidewalks
Trash for bandages

Ran-down shacks
Crumbs meant to be thrown away

People scream, violent greys
With rugged impressions
As they walk wearily, faintly
Impatiently

Half-dead men fleeing their caskets
Just existing is the ambition

Light blue azure
Hover about

Kid's naïve
Vanish
When a loud car yields

Azure II

Headed towards dusk
-but first let me inhale deeply and exhale
And control myself
Settle down beast…ok
I shall indulge

Headed towards dusk that illuminating sparkle
Have found its home
In my eye
Dilated pupils

Oh this is quite riveting
But hide
Settle down
And hide behind
The jewel, that crept
It's way inside my eyelids

Why all the drama
Well…
Let me indulge

The azure was quite different
Awakening before eve
The ocean, on the coast
Was watching to
But it envied the azure

The azure,
Light blue,
With a purple haze
With pink precious ribbons

Delightful
And the orange eye
Set in the west reflecting
Its rays to make a
Orange ejaculation

Orange
Subtle
The sun was humble
It looks moist

Like he was about to cry
But cheer up
Your tears
Create joy on the desolate canvas

That worries below

The stars were impatient
Impulsive, but no my shining friends
It's the azures turn

Oh you was light blue in the east
But in the west you were wild

How pitiful
The walking upright creatures
Didn't notice
You're angelic
Maximum
Potential

The azure had planes in the sky
Trying its best to get close to you
But
It can't

So it leaves or shall I say exhale
Its white catastrophe
In the air
Trying to decorate

But what nonsense
Man!
Planes!

I'm already
Sensible
Lost with my feeling
That can't be explained

So don't cloud my vison
With your blunders

Oh azure,
You make me feel
Like…

Oh azure I apologize let me not
That'll be selfish of me
To
Express

And take away from your beauty
To focus on me

The man speaks

Let us be honest,
The man is in heat
To himself, amative, amorous
Man is frantic when the goddess appears

Let us not boast about the red tears
That we are so scared to shred

The elephant is scared of mice

Comedy it appears, but vulnerability is right
The elephant in heat is dangerous
He is the king on a rampage,
What's in his heart is...

Female
Mating
I myself
Am scared sometimes

A boy,
An orphan
Looking for his mother
Man...

We'll you'll laugh
Vulnerable
But in heat at 19

Our minds drive us to
Tides
Waves
Rivers
Rugged mountains
And plays Russian roulette
With ourselves

Trying to calm down
And have some sort of control
We look
For…

Dark ravines
And look for the winds
To tickle us
And fondle us…

Gently…

Publicly known…

All of this
-for a woman
Who is known to decorate
Life

…with her perfume
And she plants seeds into our mind
And it takes root
And when we grow tired
And weary

"It"…

The plant or flower
Decides to blossom on our beds…
And
Pleasure
Pain
Insomnia

Takes place
And our feast is still in our stomachs

Can I say boldly?
I go to sleep easy
Without embroidering
In my head…

The vison
Of today's woman

I must admit
This abstinence stains
A quiet beast
But…

When she waltzes around
Giving me
The teasing eye

I still have to remember
I have to go to sleep tonight

Transcending towards him (Bus Ride)

My head hanged on a glass window
Secluded in blue cotton seats
In a therapeutic stupor
My mind was numb
My face was
Motionless

Emptying
Today's burdens
Through my stare
That's covered by black
Narcotic lenses

I looked out and seen tragedy
Shakespearean plays
With gullied actors…
Unaware!

My
Mobile heaven
I dreamt in the sunlight's
Gleam with my eyes open
Almost drunk off of self-imposed hypnosis
I sat in peaceful insomnia

Bus driver…

Take me where you want…

Because,
I cannot
Bear to get off

...Proceed

Mellow day
The azure
Was dormant
Maybe saving or consuming energy
For the night time spectacle

Nothing entertaining
The sun hiding
Behind
Quiet dull clouds

The white beds were daydreaming
About
Tomorrows
Brightness

As for me
The librarian boy
Sitting on the steps
With a twinkle in my eye

Ready to
Free
The beast
With the pen

So
Intricately
I
Write

Fairytale to you

A chilly
Languor
Spring evening…

A muse sat in a rough corner
Of a forbidden breezeway
Yielding to the azure
With the screeching
Call
Of amative birds

Who has taken flight to
Go to
The gathering
Of the multitudes of birds

Who took lay
In the promiscuous orgy

He sat on two steps by a wooden fence
Inhaled three deep
Curls of oxygen
Hurting
His nostrils
With the alcoholic
Beverage
Madame Nature
Can only provide…

Trying to get sedated
Off the senses
He was reconciling with nature
Since their departure

Was
Long
Forgotten

Since childhood frolicking
And sensational dreams
…
He sat quietly
Entertaining himself

The medicine
That needs to be taken
To see
The scrotum
Of the dusk…

And once
Indulged
He turns into
The mystic beast

That
(You) reader
Will get mystified
By
And
Envy
His very being

Treasure in the desert

Welcome

I wandered on sacred deserts
Mojave
Saharan
Biblical deserts

In the heat
Searching for
Ven-
Or
Ev-

Ahh

I was panting like a dog
Searching for the erotic bone
Hoping to experience
The orgiastic rapture

But not at all
I cannot
Find the treasure
That is hidden

That fertile
Treasure…
Which if I find,
My fleshly log
Will
Thrust
In
And out
Violently

Joshua Victor

Like furious
Winds
And innocent
Wind chimes

But no
My mouth dry
My urge
Grew subtle

And then...

A black hole
Subsided in the sand
I fell in without screaming
As if,
I knew
It was coming

The haunting solace
Foretells
In the black abyss
Where
Sullen
Demons
Were
Angels

I was quiet,
Renouncing
My search

Well obviously
My bottom
Occupied

Black rocks
And I perched up
On the wall
Sweating
Drinking
A bowl of
Fowl juices
The ghouls prepared

My feeling
Was numb

Numb
Sitting

Breathing
I
The
Muse

So selfish
And conceited
I reproached this madness
Of ignorant vanity

Then a wind
Of dust
And
Sand swept
Down the abyss

Causing the demons to flinch
The sand in the sunlight
Had
My vision
Obscured

What the hell is going on?

My heart was ahead of me
Beating
Feverishly
Nervously
It was screaming

The search!
…but I'm still
Confused

What is this?

Echoes!
I hear faintly

A green
Fertile vine
Poured
Down

I grabbed it
Hesitantly

Ahh my erotica
Eternity
And right
Before
I came
Out

A pale
Hand
With two veins
And a soft feel
Like fleshly sheets
Wrapped around my wrist

I looked up
In awe…
Softly
Murmuring…

Venus!

Joshua Victor

White!

I heard a pleasant surge
My ears was
Ordaining
A noetic feeling
Running
Furiously in my nerves
Inside birds can be calm
Wandering freely
Without worrying…

About a sinister wretch
Or
Scavenger
Crippling them with fear

And their memories
Foreshadows
Them
To eat
Their
Food quick
While digesting paranoia

I seen languorous doves
Whose beaks
Were gnawed
By white fingers
Of a hazy delight

A kid's laugh echoes eternally
A rabbit, hopping fearlessly
Into a fervor oasis
Where his heart flowed freely with water

I seen a woman
Whose limbs
Were relaxed
Where
The flowers tickled her feet

And the soil had seeped into her back
Making
A bed for
Her aching back

A sensible woman
Whose nerves
We're marching with white shoes
With smooth heels…

A white blouse, was her
Orgiastic costume
And gentle winds
Made her hair flower

Moaning loudly

Bees
Wonder curiously

About the fleshly nectar
That is on top of the lilies
Nothing familiar to them

A fox
Sated
By a gentle
Human

Whose
Memory
Tainted aggression

The sun watching
The spectacle
Watching it all

The muse silently cries
Tears
Of
White epiphanies

Moon of my bohemia

I looked up and…
I
Strolling down the vacant road
Where creatures feet were music to my ears

The wind expressing,
Cold chills was furious
Because my scarf choked my neck

..Dark blue night with a setting of ghost
Strangers waltz creepy in the night

A hollow world…

I looked up
And seen a silhouette
Living
With grey pores

A sphere
Suspended
In attractive, sensibility
White
Dreamy…

Like a circular rock
Or pale flesh
Calling to a dream
Or naïve gaze

A hallucination?
No!
My head is clear

Is it...
The moon of my bohemia

Deranging
My ambitions
Capture me
Performing coitus
With my soul

It was calling me
And my eyes
Were fixed
On this circular
Illuminating
Light

That lit up my hollow evening
I tried
To free myself
Into the rapture
Of where wolves pity
Creatures who busy
With worldly troubles

My my my this light
In the dark
Blue
Azure

Had my behavior
Moving
Manifesting
What surge

Why
Oh moon of my bohemia

I stared
Wanting
The ocean

I stared
At
The
Blue Norwegian dreams

A dog
Examining
Gentle strangers

The moon
The moon

Oh my azure
But
The moon
Subsided

Just to make
Its presence
Known
To me

Have you seen…
Unnecessary burdens
Floating in my heart
So all you wanted
To do
Was make them
Disappear

With your
Posture
And loud
Appetite

Were you
Cultivating
Flowers
Of a black nectar
That only you can
Tend to
And
Never
Bees

You was taking advantage
Of my attention
Knowing my tentative
State

And I'm here
Naked
Caught up
In a mystery

Free
Myself
Through your
Dark entrapment
That tickles my heart

The voice

The voice
Was alluring
Enchanted in
A subtle fervor

A high
Indulging
Song

Ecstatic
And amative
Feminine…
Her
Breathing

In between words

A beautiful canyon
With a quiet gap in between
But an invisible
Orgy of a bridge

If you squint
Your eyes
Only dreamers
Can see

But
It is
What I hear

A child's voice
A young woman's voice

Whose or which was echoing
Absorbing chambers
The elating
Seducing
Drawing in
A naïve
Innocent
But weary
Voice

The words
Were ideal
A vibration
Of woman
Luring me in

Because
The desolate external
Bothered me

But
Her voice
Was getting faint
Then the voice ceased
And no more
Was my ears
Entertained

Recluse I

Comfortable while strolling
A calm vice grip
Enraptured
My head

The sun hiding
Behind gray melancholic
Thick clouds
Sleeping in its brightness

Wind
A voluptuous earth
Exhaling
Sensible
Breaths

Hold my hand
Caressing
My palms
And wrist
To
And
Fro

No grip
To feel
Its pulses
Smiles
On benevolent creatures

Hiding their
Dark deeds
In their black pastures

Just smile for today
And
Erase
Reflections of unforgettable winters

Because of spring
Multitudes
Of childlike acorns
With
Frolicking
Brown bug leaves

Moving
Scattered on the ground
The fragile moves
Gliding while walking

Secluded by a vacant
Brown building
Noisy boisterous
Streets

Just to eat
A quick
Snack

The secret

Frozen we become
Drawn in we become lost

Picasso don't look at me
Don't be vindictive

Artist listen
Observers pay attention

We all get drawn in
Like gullible children
Looking at murals of
Colorful fervor
Vigorous
With flamboyant
Ambitions

All of us indulging ourselves
In the pictures of the great
Hoping
To numb ourselves

And dreaming
Of mystical intentions
Hoping our lives can be
Identical to myths

Brought about by
The slumber beast
That some of us can
Awake at infinite times eternally

Without
Insinuating journey
Through the mural who is
A teacher

And
Red sage
And a mirror
Who's finding comedies in our lives

Where the beast roams freely
Like a gentle exorcism
And the azure
Frothing at the mouth
While we require
An environment of
Meekness and discernment
Of angelic silence to translate
Into a picture
-art

Is something we dwell in
And go to for a bondage we desire
So the anti-social endeavors
Doesn't burn pains into the hole
In our
Hearts

Screaming
Fix it

Art
The lonely man's drug

Is bereaving medicine
That the multitudes call genius
But
Really

The beast
Awakes and
Create anger
And more

But
Let the artist kill me
For telling forbidden secrets

I'll continue later

My race

I am from
A superior race

Who foretells
Your hopeless endeavors
By looking at tricolored azures
And fields of lilies who screams

Mysticism of panorama

Whose foundation is,
The mundane world
I stared at grey clouds who taught
Me the rhetoric's of sensibility

Coupled
With
Sensitive thoughts

I know your sway and your words
Because the sun's rays
Scatter your secrets
Into the hazy air

That is obscure for him
Or her
Put plainly in the open
For us

My race

I constantly find myself
In the rapture of omnipotent fields
Whose soil is home for vacant bodies,
But that's okay

My race is reptiles
Whose scales are mirrors for humans,
Who just kick around seashells,
Not knowing its embroidering their tombstones

Wow
Let us get a glimpse
Of the subterranean village
That has us in the cradle

But we neglect
Because our vestige minds
Has encircled around naïve festivities
That been brought about
Because

-my race

Eternal
I scream eternal
As I walk through blue roads
Who lead to a golden Mesopotamia,

Whose door is black,
But it burns
As you touch the door knob
But only

My race

Can withstand the pain

My erotica

Woman
With a glare in my eye
I will be under the erotic spell
Guarded with a sacred lust

That might be blasphemy
Or sacrilegious

My eye
Will be pulsating
Beating with red fervor

Ill succumb to the feeling
Of bereaving pleasure
For the spirit
Within
Has took
Control

Ill eye you down
With the dagger
That
Killed
Caesar

My eyes scroll
Like a glass marble
On a pivot
…the black luminous holes

Will see your head
And your
Hair
That swing freely

With your rotating sway
And your feminine omnipotence
That embellishes your hips
The dress that constricts your fleshly
Pillars
Of thighs

Robust love
And a torrid desire
My palms cant grip
And your breast gentle

Smooth
Filled with the nectar
Of life
Fertile, voluptuous

Ill secretly creep up behind you
Whose intentions are to shatter mirrors,
With loud screams

I'll take my hands
Gripping tightly around your neck
That veins and blood flow
With the water of love

And my fingers
Will tickle
Down the belly
On a road
Who leads to a bush,
That protects a fertile oasis
And ill gently open the fleshly curtains
Of a symphony

And pick you up
And my monster
Will sense the maestro
(Who's so timid to perform)

And ill plunge deep
Into you my girl
And your stomach
Will flinch with ardor

Your eyes will travel behind
A black toxic curtain
Who struggles,
To see the real world

Trembling
Orgiastic earthquake
Your body will
Consume eruption

From the hot
Moist
Volcanoes
Whose
Hot lava
Trickle
Down
My
Leg

In April...it was raining and cold

Oooo I went strolling down the roads,
Grey clouds
A child screams
God cries

And cold

His tears pouring
The clouds,
Sad and streams
Hits the pavement
Roads
A thin sheet covered me

For a person
Insinuating
Endeavors
Too comical

How joy turned
To melancholy
The damp roads were fertile

Lazy, agile
Trees
Hurting
And their trunks screaming
For moist subterranean torrid water

That was burdens
Slouched over
So grey…

Subtle
The greens
And browns
On lively,
Vivid
Robust…

The only colors tending
To my heart

Automobiles
Slippery
Rubbery wheels
Multitudes of rushing ambition
Crashing
Splashing

His tears
That makes noise
Of a subtle,
Screams

I walked closest
To the sidewalk
My feet plunging
Into the roads

Where my shoes were barricades
To the shallow water
Threatening my toes

Oh the fervor!
Of the cold water
I feel tempting me

Teasing
My feet that's protected
Inside

Oh I was in oasis
Cold and protected
Vertigo
To the tears of him

Are dripping
So politely
Softly on my back
Wiping away invisible bruises

Trying to deflower
My fleshly pores

No
Are they speaking,
Relentlessly to the muse
Who struts with a stupor?

Who thrust his fist,
Into pockets
To emphasize
An obscure vision
And enhancing the sense of hearing

Head bowed low
Multitudes of illuminating lights
Moving sarcastically
Hysterical
Reflecting off of roads

A double mirror
That moves

What wrinkles,
Floating towards a destination
Complementing
Brown moist streets

That's
Parallel
To eyes who are stuck

My walk is bent
On an obscure sense of ordaining
Rain
Who calls up the...

Trees who's slouched over
Who shall the stampede,
Ordain successfully
On this grey day
Of ardor

Experiment of haikus

Rays through cracked blinds
No mood no movement

Tired long day
Frozen drink with happiness

A cat stare
A stranger flinches

Gossip and laughing
Scurry while walking

Quiet death
So many people around

Futile, frivolous
Trivial, but it has to make sense

Marks! What are they?
Made by a human

Interpretation?

Quiet...that was all

I
For hours
Words
Were renouncing

They couldn't find the obvious treasure
That was sealed by
My lips

And the spring was not agitating
Nor aggressive
By a silent sustained torment
Was all it was swinging

A Friday where the leaves
Roam the sidewalks
Hesitantly

And even cats were curious
About the forbidden silence

The birds look here and there
Enjoying the panoramic view
Delighting themselves

Were the
Creatures
Hidden in undesirable houses?

Automobiles
Sat still
Haunting…

And
Sun
Looking for
At least adolescents

Wow
My friend
I guess I'll take a shower
Of perfumed humid,
Steam

While I'll get
In the state
Of vigor
And pensiveness

To see why it's so calm

And how
Nostalgia
Build its foundation

While the shadows of noise
Have yet to pass by

Find me

The winds will hurl
The phenomena in the air
Hastily

Listen closely
Pay attention
To determine
Where it's showing you

What way to embark?

Do not struggle or chastise
Just follow

The butterfly will be your guide
Vermilions
And beds of flowers
Black silhouettes with pink cushions

Inside will be signs
But listen and follow

The winds who howls
The Dionysian wolf
Naked and fertile
You shall be

A daze is your ecstatic concentration
Walk hesitantly
With love

Golden pebbles
Tickle your feet

And don't lose sight of
The gay butterfly
The silent finger will lead you
To a brown cave

Screaming,
Who's worthy to go near?

Enter in
Friend where
The jubilant aqua lights
Barricades the walls

Where spiders
And bats
Lay
And take siege

There you'll find

The box
(in Spanish)
Open love bird

Inside you'll see a brown manuscript
Tainted
With ancient
Mysticisms
And it reads…

"For the one who discovers
Run
For the one who discovers
Rages
Run with fervor
And renounce your human passions
Seek the beast who destroyed me
Never die in nostalgia
But live in
Famine of desire

I need not see the same
Many nymphs stand still"

-Joshua victor
To you

The night tells

When the bitter hour of dusk strikes
And deeds and endeavors go stale
The spirit of emptiness and omnipotent disdain
Intertwines with the nectar of lust

And the moon bereaves

And how much of a paradox it is to see
You
Moon whimper over me

When night times quietness
Takes roots in your ears
Like unpleasant seeds
Whose roots
Get nutrients from your brain

The thoughts of naked fairies
And pleasure
Eternal
And busted valves
Where white musty dew
Drips down the sheets
From violent thoughts
Of a orgiastic
Memorabilia

Let Raphael
Or Picasso
Make
Mona Lisa scream

And her tears pierce
Her face
From pleasure

Oh Mona

My inspiration
Open your mouth

And sigh from a long day
And let me plant seeds in your mouth
Sinister woman of Dionysius

Let me look
In your yellow eyes
And see your urge
So I can puncture
That eternal wound
That's meant to get filled
With the nectar of Casanova

Almost...defeated

My soul shaking with vigor
Some red ardent mistress
Married my heart
Internally inside was eternal vibration

My nerves
A wild ecstatic exorcism
The beast was panting like a dog
Waging his tale

What creature
Shall be dormant?
Who shall sleep?

The stroke right before midnight
The fertility of this ecstasy was innocent
My soul stolen from me
Placed on top of Venuses white wing

Inside I sing rhymes
And notes

Love was screaming
Survive gentle child
Red oasis dripping
Oh Venus I'm mild

Corrosion of wee…
My head barely floating
On top of the sea
Or sensual aggravation

Only the burgeoning love of intention
Kept me above water
Or else frantically
I would have sunken

Drowning
The muse could have been dead
By a brown rustic anchor
Because too quick he fell

How naïve

Bubbles
Of sensitivity of a woman
Will float out of his mouth
And pop

And a fisherman
Thinking it was seafood
But in vertigo
He could have been in

Not knowing
It was a dead seer
At the bottom of the sea
Because of a seducing truth

How erotic and gentle
How embarrassing the obituary
What will be written,
On his tombstone

Deeper to where

Footsteps sunken in the sand
I walk cautiously
Like a child walking in the dark
Trying to find the light

Nervous with a fever…
Slowly I stride,
Where my tongue is Velcro
To the roof of my mouth

I thirst,
Cat eyes looks at me with disgust
Teasing, and of a temperamental, quietness,
Winds blow grains in my eyes stale and burning

Where is my oasis?
Sacred
Brown shirt torn on my chest
Fondled and caressed by dry sediments

My grimace
The snake
The viper
Circles my feet

My trapeze guide
Green
Scales of hope
Black wounds
On yellow plates
Pink ribbon
Out his mouth hissing…

"Go oh child
Deeper
Deeper
I'm your guide"

Heavenly serpent
Don't trick me
But give me cold vinegar
To silent the temptation

The azure
Oh what do you care,
If I fall on my knees
And…

(La muerte of the muse)

Visit from the mystic paladin

So a host
Hollow inside
A human tent
Where the soul is dull

A jubilant echo
He hears faintly
The wardrobe
Black

Concealing a demon to a norm…

But in a stupor
With a hollow mind
He feels suspended
On electric wires

And his toes
And feet
Balancing on a fierce
Mural

Two inches in width
Tickling his nerves

Yet he's still

Now
For a visit from the mystic paladin

Oh host!
your empty
Perfect for the black embodiment
Oh how black pearls
That is ample and robust fill the vacant canister

Enters in your body
Some force or medium
What spirit is this?

A dark passion
Conquers the soul
That thirst
How can you conceal this power?

Who shall sustain
This body
That is now filled with an erotic knight

Your senses heightened

Some steam from a nubile chimney
Too hot to contain
Let alone eat from the pot so soon
Your eyes are bulged with a feeling of being alert

Test thy spirit now

Immortal you feel
Can you sense the thought of another human?

Oh host of fearlessness
Can you detect today's pain
That seldom gets talked about
And most likely repressed
And banished

But your sharp ears
Gets it as soon as you hear a voice
You sense the biography

Oh tell me host,
Can you draw people in your rapture,
So easily where they don't know where's the exit
Or door

To free them from this chaotic bondage
Of freedom
Would a conversation hinder an action,
And foretell a night's endeavor

Can you host,
Conquer the dream
Of a bereaving woman
Who shows disdain towards her situation,
And clothed herself with a costume of jubilee

Self-medication

Oh beautiful host
I scream,
What powers do you have?
Where those black jewels,
Is penetrating souls
And a connectedness
Or beastly food
That never
Gets noticed
On gold plates
Where black flowers
Are
Embroidered
In the silverware

Joshua Victor

What food!

Oh mystic paladin
Conquer me please

Take me away on your back
And float away with me
Into the obscure haze that dissipates
Right before dawn

Bye bye butterfly

You see butterfly,

You'll become frivolous
Even the black silhouette
Where your yellow color of wings
(Feeling that's piercing to the child's eye)
Have to,
Become mundane

You're pure,
Butterfly
I know as a child
I was happy and sated
To see you tickle my skin
That's like the touch of the little girl

That holds my hand and run
And I'm force to frolicking and play

With sincerity and mildness
To see you flap your wings,
And like a leaf flicker
When the sunlight causes you to change
Spontaneously

As you float in the air
Gently, whose destination is the branches,
That so ever lies in a slumber of an arc
Where your feet balance

And your pretentious nature
Is to walk
Like the male peacock

Fluctuating
In front of the female
During mating

Oh,
How treasures like you is kept in a diary
Or a secret with preponderant mysteries

But over time my friend,
You bore me
And embarrass me

So what inspiring muse,
Shall my eyes cast bewitching spells on now?

Oh
It is
The
Moth

Your dark cousin
Of a full moon
The disdain is embellished
For his nocturnal departure

You see,
Unlike you butterfly
Me myself
Isn't flamboyant

But
Your cousin
Understands me

Your stagnant inside!

But
Your cousin desires

Caves and celestial light
By any means
The line he flies' in to see the light
Despite his suffering

He risk
Getting killed because of his color
Gray
Dark
Black
Pleading melancholy

So he goes towards light
Saying
"Who shall kill me here?"
While committing treason
To your conscience and tortured soul

Oh moth,
I love you
Marry me

And at midnight
We can both fly towards the light
In endless night
And let my hands be a boat
For your sacred voyage

Recluse II

Sound asleep,
Exulting silence
Where toes taps the tile floor
Crackling

But this time I'm in my room
Stuffy and small
The white walls is a barricade for inducing dreams
And cars take heavy strolls down vacant weary roads...

I wonder
Are these passengers planning orgy
Destruction
Or solemn sleep?

Either from work
Or the tragedies of wine

Either way
Secluded,

Secluded
From everything
Where my heavy body
Suppress the corner of my bed

Writing fine verses

I'll have to recline in the bed
And my head, cushion on a cold pillow
Where the blood of my passions boils
The food of mysticism and dreams
Ready to be taken off the inducing oven
And away
My soul will
Fly

Entering the other world
Hypnotically

By red eyes

I have to say
What would be my last thought?

Staring...and staring some more

My black jewelry
Circular onyx
On top
Of a white pearl sphere

These voluptuous stones
One out of the five senses

I stared
I stared sharper than a lumberjack ax
I could see through the sheet
That was invisible
And fluorescent

And I found eternal breath

I escaped
Running with the child of death
A stare...

So piercing and penetrating
I have found the roots
Of planted jewels
Where every panner missed

I mean the scattered skulls
That was home for the taboo,
Architecture
So this stare was the sinister brother of scrutiny
Where one loses concentration

And gets lost in the scream
Of frantic, elated birds,
No longer could I decipher
Abstract day
Marries my soul

(Sir what do you mean)

I mean monsieur,
Definition
And trivial interpretation
Have met its match

I mean you scientists
And creeds
Of egoistic molecular
Secretly are dubious

I mean my soul
Was testifying
Sun
Wind
Trees
Clouds

And...I don't know

One's eyes,
Must be possessed
To get to a picture of vivid obscurity

Tears from unknown taverns
Unknown scattered reasons
Found the focal point of my eyes
And surprised me
I am off guard
And unaware of the fertility of nature

The ominous feeling
Oh the outside show!

Animals with the winds are the horns
And commanding officers
On the fertile battlefield
The sparrows are my commander
I'm in the battle
Where armor is guarded
By sensible guns
That shoots
Streams of blood
That nectar gets its sweet taste from

My plan in this war
Is to make it to my bed
Safe,
Without losing balance
By traveling through my chamber
Of regenerating hallways

Cheating

My head was lying down flat
-on a black table
Preparing myself for sensible latitudes
My ears were getting entertained, tickling!

I tell you dear reader
-I was cheating
I was like a peasant, performing
Espionage on the king and mistress
Doing away with each other

So I hear breathing, feet tapping, and impatient shaking knees
…what sounds that was exposed
I was cheating…reader
I was cheating…

The child

Who shall say I am this?
Or he must be that?

Stop the frivolous bickering
(Usually the sparrows
Who premeditates on top of the street lamps)
Can tell you

But since it's another evening
And the midnight is awakening slowly
In its slumber
I'll tell you

I am the boy whose almond eyes
Find his mother
Bereaving
Loving…
Sleeping
Complaining
Or aching with pain
Who laughs
At her children slightly
And loud
While feeling unbearable
Sinister pain
That she has in a docile shell of a cradled life
Steady…

At the same time in my hands are epistles
And epochs of a gothic,
Evil of languorous pleasure

Whose ecstasy
Is enraptured
Whom its first word begins with
The word of the dove
Whose eyes and beaks foretell
A sudden
Fertile…crypt

I am a child who talks
With a poignant sound that elevates to a
Childs pitch while laughing and screaming
With merry frolicking through the halls

Because the rays of sunshine
Through the blinds are calling…

Whose solitude is an empty painful,
Canister where pure distilled water can fill
By stains inside, at adhesion to steal
But it don't effect the water

And dents and bruises on the outside
Is self-inflicted with confidence

I am a child who seeks travel
Who seeks pleasure through lonesome stroll,
Holding hands with green mother
Who takes care of me alone

But pleasure
-and a girl?

I'll find here!
If the twilight in her eyes
Is dripping an eclipse
Dreamy
In my heart
That's touched by equinox,
Of black water that's nourishing

I am the child who wants not a funeral
But ashes scattered in a cave
Or desert
Or in a lake

Where leviathan sleeps
So when he sees it
His fangs gleaming,
Through his smile…
Because…

The child
Has returned to the sea

Red dog

A dog
Who haven't played with a toy,
Or some wooden "thing"
Or an empty can

In which his fangs
Can plunge into piercing
With vengeful appetite
Hating the waiting
Finally seeing
What he can chew

So he is enraptured with aggression
And puncturing
Shredding

So the dog
Tugging with the fervor
From his jaw and neck
And whose fangs gnaws and punctures

But holds in place
And paws for a grip
Leverage

Tugging and pulling
Losing the tempting knots
And stretching out

This
"Chew thing"

His head
To and fro
Shakes violently
Left and right
Around like the moon
Spun on some mystic finger

His head squirming
Violently
Until
The "chew thing"
Is exposed

Loose
And shredded

-so
Like that
My lady

I'll be…

Until,
I see you faint in exhaustion
Which you would have busted
Leaking,
Like some attractive fountain
That has been forgotten
Because no one seen the cracked hole
At the bottom

Unveiled

Unveiled
Vulnerable
The forbidden secrets will never...
No more suffocate under a blanket

That can easily be docile wardrobe
In society

Every endeavor
Secret
Passion
Dream
Sin
Evil
And grotesque hunger roams freely

Without pondering
Or pensiveness

Let us reveal these sadistic epochs

I noticed you want to lie
Oh treacherous
Fertile woman
With your loins exposed
And some young stiff man
Causing sacred commotion between your gates of legs
Thrusting with ardor
With a puncturing arrow from sacred Indians

That invokes
Visions and dreams

Ecstasy
Moaning and groaning

Like a distant mermaid
Screaming loudly

As you wish to see
You're tormented ex-lover
How that will ripen you in the mood

How you wish to stare deeply in his eyes
Like a black water of a sprite in the eternal deep well
How you want to kill him with your stare showing,

"Look old lover
I have found a man
That can puncture my wound till it bleeds
The honey and burgeoning nectar from blossoming buds"

How much joy for this
Orgiastic malevolence

What about you dear brother
With your pensiveness of violence

How you want to murder ex-lovers
In a cold sweat
And bulging eyes

And how you premeditate
Devouring
This woman eternally
In some eternal rapture

Where demons and wolves draw near
Peaking in windows to see you mimic them

Inside your ardent Venus

Hellacious how your disdain and malevolence
Screams for her "former",
How you drive to have her burn her nostalgia
And her past with your violent outspoken
Upheaval core

Shifting her internal body in some frenzy
While she cries tears of red
And you don't stop until the demon and the animal
Grow weary

You think not of human
While you're intruding her
But let us grow barbaric and sinning
While stimulating her

I also sense her secret again
Teasing and talking

You are nothing to her
(So she portrays on stage)
Trying not to get adhesive towards you
(But inside never ending ripples of a lustful river
That never slackens)

Until the monster sink-in his talons
Or trunk for a drink
It burns inside
Heavy liquid wax burning her intestines

Where she tries to fill the holes
With patches of trivial talks
But look closely
To see the holes

What games has the Vikings made
And the heretics of the barbarians

Where love and passion dictates
The liquid ingredients that gets mixed
Simultaneously, only to boil
On the precious stove

Until the steams flows
Through the room

Get enchanted
Day after day
Oh what bitter secrets
We try to hide…

That lies open
In front of
Venus and diony-

So funny and comical
We think were clever

Unknown

By a river,
Boredom was the tyrant
That took siege upon the throne

Skipping rocks
A child
Killing time
Till I see him in a tombstone

Like a tom thumb
Or simpleton
I seen
The rocks bouncing off the water

Like reflecting
Motile crystal
Bursting like
Liquid smithereens

How it tickled my heart

-what is that flinching?

I pondered
As some boat with green haze
Makes the passenger or passengers obscure

This boat
With a green delight of smoke
This madness,
Tempting me to run

But my senses held me in the clutch

It drew near

A curvaceous
Figure
Woman!

Closer
Closer
My heart jumping
Like a canon during the days of war and rebellion

But I restrained
This woman looked at me floating by
Gliding,
Where nature and Shakespeare intertwined together

And a presentation
Unreal
And quasi mystical

Oh,
I see this woman with a green dress
Transparent where her body was seened
Her hips were swaying like fertile fleshly,
Wind Chimes left and right like knives

(If your face was near)

Like a curtain on top of a goddess
Lifts discreetly with teasing winds
Her bosoms like cushions of a circular bag
Where sprinkled sand occupied
And nipples
Taunting
Alluring
Like some precious target
For flesh spears to pierce

Her arms cross like a wrap,
Around Christmas boxes
Each hand mingling
Her fingers together

Her hair black
Like the nights drink poured on her scalp
And stained her sweet vines, to her shoulders

Her brown eyes like a circular mural
Dripping amber into my heart
Her lips like a red sleeping butterfly on the side,
Pungent and filled up with blood

-she whispers

I couldn't tell

She draws near
And reaching out as if she found prey
Grabs me

By my brown stained shirt
Ancient
Some hand-me down rags
And pulls me in her boat

Without a word

I inches away from her face
Puckered up and she…
My eyes closed and she…

Where is her silent response?
I open them up…

And there I was
Skipping rocks
By a river
Eyes towards the sky
And some bird flew over me

Dropping a note

And I confused
For unknown reasons
Waltzing towards the paper
And it reads…

"My love did you doubt
Oh Joshua you froze
I am who I am
Close your eyes"

Who she is

Late night
Where night owls make preparations
And pensive festivities
My room dark, absent of all light

My cracked blinds
Maneuvers the moonlight through,
Reflecting off my window pane
And the carpet

I lie quiet
Renouncing
What I thought was known
In some mystic boat,

Denouncing
What I thought was prophetic,
Fertile thoughts

My heart was telling the truth like revealing
Secret languages from some manuscript,
Which forces the soul to cease,
So my mind had to yield

I lie quiet
Renouncing the lies that I so
In anguish thought,
My thoughts were beguiled

But no conjuring
But beguiled
Thinking I was right

O wretch of the moonlight
You were wrong
And the midnight nymph's
Hysterically laugh

But
Without
Bursting out
In anger I was
Calm
Tranquil
Serene

I…
I…
Accepting her for who she is

Poison burns

My dear romantic peers
I'll be honest
What is this black well,
That screams

Murmuring echoes
Of tears of steal
Why can such a hole with nothing in it
Cause so much pain

My nostalgia is teasing,
Tempting me to go furious

The beast half full with no food left
So he contemplates about eating dung or dust

Soothing is a quick burst of euphoria
That has us leaking like,
Melancholic fossils
Without ceasing

Who shall be bold to drown in the waters,
Of fervor
Where some weary nuisance floats without life
No desolate shore is on the way

My black moth sits on my finger
Envying me
Because our dark paths lessen
As I madly scourge the day for true light

I mean night of engraved,
Words that's embroidered
In our eternal tombstones since birth

My mother without a clue haven't warn me
About such heartaches
Where the beating continues only with a puncture
Agile,
And it stains with some poison that sting

Boiling in quick bursts
That one feels
And pupils dilate in light rooms
Because darkness inside has cause
Them to search frantically for light

I'm an honest man searching for sand,
That slowly seeps in my hands and melts
Tickling passages through my rough ashy fingers

How I take a compulsive dive
Like some groundhog in winter
With red fangs and a smile that's camouflage
With a grimace because underground,
Closer to the core
Brings him rapture of pleasure

Oh how I think the molten lava
Burns coolly down here

Desperate

You see,
I'm
up late in my bedroom
Pulling my hair
And grinding my teeth

With yellow eyes
Of seldom remorse
Because I have coated
Reconstructed thoughts to please myself
And sustain gray tears
Of docile whisperings
That screams

Look,
The orphan is all by himself
With a tight hand to grip his own

I understand the mind of animals
Is survival
As mine is to
But the breaths I take
Rings thoughts of love
Or not
Like some cliché falling pedals
Off some wrinkled red rose

Joshua Victor

You who are naïve and so easily pleased
I call you to write down scripture
So I can plant them in your heart
And ill steal your joy

While ill frantically
Run through fields of flowers
Where black thorns
Prick the sol of my jagged feet

The apology

I must apologize with a subtle voice,
A ghost is quiet making noise if you hear,
The quiet wind sneaks underneath,
The cracked door

Excuse me while ill ride on the spirit of lunar,
Snake,
To the sublime exodus
Of nocturnal realms
By which
The white door is suspended in the air
How mystical

That its foundation
Is immovable,
With no foundation

I tried walking with my weary camel there,
Eternal waiting,
Like some Black dog waiting,
For his gentle owner to bring road kill

I walk down the white line in bright day,
With preponderant screeching of the birds
And the bass buzzing of wings rubbing together
Where the desert sun murders my body,

With a frivolous passion

To take siege on the road,
Just to get a drink
Or free myself out of the prison
Of boredom

Where grey prison walls manifest itself
On the pink,
Triumphant roads…

To conquer dreams

I must say to conquer dreams,
Is telling scarce white Siberian tigers,

"I understand your mystical eyes"

That screams yellow intertwined with orange
Reminiscent of a fortuneteller's crystal ball,
Who can calm the enmity of the tiger with his stare,
And not tremble violently,
Feebly,

Without their sunken hearts falling to their guts
Like some delicious piece of food
The topping of sweetness

Oh I cry out,
With the black desolate hole
The romantic,

Whose only hope is to see the fairy or mystical nymph
Who so teasingly shows us the worlds
Icarus
(Well at least to where he was flying)
That can be attained through relentless debauchery
And unyielding travel

Who shall roam?
The sprites of night
Until the sun who opens his eye
And peaks at the muse of night and spit
Orange, purple, and pink smoke
At his back, warning him to sleep
Because he'll show all his endeavors
To common repetitive crowds,

Who thinks monotony
Is handsome and talented
Like Mozart,

What sickness…

So I guess his only channeling,
While being stubborn and still
Is to be enchanted and possessed by green demons
Who's to demanding, only when writing verses

Or a long day of some labor,
Pensive behavior needed to be figure out

Ideal,
He hope as with a child
Finding some delicious candy after being bad

To stumble in the shower
Head hung low
Like heavy blooming flowers
And see the metal head of Poseidon
And hot steam
Streams,
Melt away burdens
And uneasy lamenting,
And stupid black mud,
From dumb,
Drunken rocks
Of work

Fall off his fleshly pores
Who screams to be clean

So I guess,
Indulging in that deeply…
-that debauchery legal?

But dammit if it's not

Falls on his bed
With a head of cold
Wet
To get on his knees
And
Pray
With ardor

To have a dream
Of a fertile stroke
That carries him away…
To realms of eternal

Bird

Black sparrow grew weary,
Bored of flight

-stagnant

Finds refuge and reclusive rest
On top of an electric pole
Where his claws grip

-he searches

For love?
Mate?
Food?
He looks
At scoundrels
Inhabitants
Well calculated
And perched

With their walkers
Dogs
And feces of expressions

(kids and adolescents)

He looks,
Oh mystic scavenger

Yielding in pensive meditation
He looks over the landscape
To see the green beds,
And grey and blue mirrors
Of electric steel moving in a sullen disposition

Grey buildings
Cathedrals
Being spied on by grey lurking azures
For a minute

Then flies away
Without warning
Far
Far away

Escape

I'll walk
(Drunken)
And I'll stumble with my black coat and white collar shirt
(A true romantic nature is the sage)

I'll walk and I will purposely leave the black vestige
Remnants to make a trail if you want to escape...

The poet who endures immense suffering
Whose only job is to find escapes through dreams,
Before dying and laid in the gothic tombstone
Whose debauchery is his panorama and teacher

It is I
Whose duty it is no matter what pain
Is to find routes to mystical treasures
Before I die and go to the sublime

I'll be the guide
And you will be forced to contemplate and dare

What am I saying?

The ideal

-and you sir…

Hmmm
Well to see the spectra of light fall upon the earth
With a fertile tone like, voluptuous springs
Or melancholic waterfalls,
Radiating so ever gently on me

To ride on beds of scattered clouds
Like the mystic chariot
Whose rider is ordained by the hostile winds
Of the azure, never ceasing
Until the blanket of eve,
Tells me to sleep

To go to the bed of Poseidon
And pick leaves from the laurels around his head
At the bottom of the sea
Where the anchors stubbornly
Want to penetrate to the core of the earth
Without succumbing to death

(Impatient nymph)

To see the pyramid,
Enchanted and golden tombs and caskets
Where the mural of Venus is embroidered
In the leaking moist gold
Like some painting done by Caspar

To see the mountains
Taunt my spirit and impress me to fear them,
To see the hand come from the sky with majesty
And the wretched mesmerizing sinister hand from the earth

Whose debris covers the skin,
Maggots, dirt seeds, and skull
Intertwine together
Just to bring the eagle near me
And grip my shoulder with its piercing talons
Like a place where he goes to stalk prey
Secretly, lucrative,

On top of a mile high boulder
How he mistakes me for nature
What debauchery and inclination I would feel
With a pinch of gratitude

To see
The snow melt
Or the lava

Or the hare searching
Tickled by the grass on his feet
Hmm will be a treat for me

But I wonder

Whose inn will support the sedated body?

The scent

On a grey, lousy bench
Stained with brown vestige
Of food, squeaking every time I think
Let alone move

Sitting like a homeless man indigenous
To falling debris from orange, dry, crackling leaves

-damned bench mocks the torture inside of me
Are you going to embarrass me any further?
You clever, depressed bench,
How ironic it is you are secluding yourself under a tree
Hiding from the sunlight's gleam

But then

I smell a fragrance
Of pungent bellflowers
Mixed, with the blossoming spring
Of a loud feminine perfume

Whose scent
That I forever search for like
A dead man's rag given to a bloodhound

I quiver like the cold on a moist lip
As if a captive been set free
From bereaving bondage

Oh
I'm ecstatic
hiding,

Fervor and amorous excitement within
Behind a shield of a grey solemn physique
As if I smelt not a thing

That scent,
Obnoxious
Pretentious
By itself simmering in the air like invisible steam
From the food of the senile cooking pot

Oh what joy!
Your fragrance turns languor impotence
Into a cage of electric stampede

Oh,
Your smell,
My senses
How it curls the hair of my nose back like skin teasing
The adverse heat of red flames

Then those golden legs
Smooth as sand mix with fossils of eureka
Dust,
That form flesh

I would ask myself
Before I approach or even look up,
To see all of her up close...

Should I calm myself down?
Or approach her with the enmity
That I have against women who turned me down
And take it out on her without remorse

Like Ophelia,
Letting go of leviathan's chains

Yearning for velvet flowers

I have yearned for eternal days
For the pink horizon to direct me
To fields of flowers that cry out melancholic cries
Who's to say that brooding evanescence is a pillow
But to sleep would be a disaster

I have rolled around the bed with her
Whose legs intertwined with mine
And whose bottom fit right in my pelvis
Like a sensual puzzle
Or cup

I have yearned for days
Where I can sit by grey tombstones
And midnight noises are embellished
By being uncomfortable

Forming the howling phantasm
That use to scare me
When gripping the hands of mother

But
There leaning against the tombstone
Like a withered bed of roses
You will see,

A muse
Whose look is searching of sweet delight,
And engraved on the tombstone
Is Arthur Rimbaud or maybe Baudelaire

Joshua Victor

I don't know
With this glass bottle in my hand
And my cologne of melancholy
I gave up…

Anyways

My vison was to obscure
While sitting underneath far clouds

Woman of the night

I was bombarded in the night
I walking wearily to my resting domain
As if I fought all the battles of Gideon
Approaching the door seeking nocturnal dreams

Plunging through my door
Lightning going through the core of the earth
-rest...my ambition

And as if a force field was there
I stopped
Scrutinizing my bed with fear and wonder,

A carcass
No...

The smell is fresh
Humid
Moist

Behind
The white veils hanging from my poles in my room
I
Seen a body

Hesitantly I sought meaning
As if pulling the curtains on practicing actors

Here

Lies this woman,
Whose garments knew of no owner
Tossed on the ground
Without a care

Her look and posture
Sated,
That I found her

Drunk
As if taken by some enchanted
Spell of erotic aroma

Is she mad?
Wrong room?

Caught in some trance
Her eyes lowering like
The subterrean sun who grows dark orange
While setting underneath far clouds
Digging its way in the sea

Her brown eyes
Looked at me
As if
I were prey
To a hungry buffalo
Of nostalgia

Her lips being tamed
By her
Pink
Tongue

Oh
Moist snake
Moving and caressing
Tempting Adam

Brown skin
And her long black hair crawling
On her shoulders
As if it were pulled roots from fertile grounds

Her neck
Looked alluring
For sinister
Erotic gripping

Soft and yielding
As if flinching
From running
Nerves

Her chest like a brown smooth
Antique wooden plate

Whose bosoms perched up
Like robust apples
Being forced to the top of brown rags
Tied tightly to preserve shape

Splendor stomach and torso
Like a flesh road meant to be driven,
Lurking hands

Her bush
The roof of her pink secreting passage
A tunnel through nerves
And sensual censure

Where her hands were frolicking
Taunting

Legs like brown pillars
Meant to support
A thrusting mate

-what are you looking at?

"Take me as I am
Moist and ripe
Enter into a squeezing grip
Whose only desire is to,
Suck out your grandfathers genes
And provide fertility to love
Punish me gently until my head seems
Heavy and my neck couldn't bear
Rip me"

-"please say no more"

An evening

(Them)
Oh yes, yes, yes

A horse and carriage
An evening dining in the most exquisites of restaurants
Whose servers are our slaves,
Drink the finest of wine
And see the finest view
From our balcony where we are
Superior
To inferior peasants

And you-

To walk around like the undead vestige,
Slowly as, if in a trance,
Mystified by grey…

Eating nothing,
But a bag of chips
Staring
Feeling
Receptive

Walking like an empty crypt
Enchanted on secluded grey roads
Cracked and broken
Trampled
Forgotten and dead

Trees hiding this unknown boy
Thinking of verses
Dreaming of sensual visions to write
On my journal of bohemian festivities

On vacant roads
Where evening suns is the second passenger

Through a war stricken city
A curse of the dead
Where seeds of imagination
Sprout and cultivate romance
Hmmm
That'll be an evening for me

Feast for hyenas

Open land,
Enraptured by the smell of death
Sinister vacancy
Feeling of hollow phantasm

Wounded and dead animals,
Embellish
The vulture's panorama

Signaling to Dionysus
To get his mother

The green have wilted away

Screeching, painful cries
Of babies throwing dark tantras
In painful prisons of purgatory

Hollow land
Where carcasses decorate
Like yellow sunflowers
And dandelions do
On childlike
Fertile
Fleshly
Moors

But
In the middle as if death planted seeds to his inheritance
Like a porcelain flower
A beautiful carcass sprouted from the ground
White porcelain claws

Or white gigantic spider
Turned on its back
Sleeping in solemn beds
Stained with red…

A skeletal vestige
Remnants of a mystical beast
Accompanying this enchanting site
Were curious hyenas

Creeping slowly as if confused
And pondering
Smelled the screaming death
Laughing hysterically
As they do

Gnawing on thirsty porcelain bones
No meat to get them full

Neither carnivore nor herbivores

Just seduced by the crypt
Digging their teeth
As if to get stronger from the carcass

Gnawing
Gnawing

Oooo
How their fangs feel good
Biting into my wounded heart

Calypso observes
(Sad phantasy)

Let the flames of his seclusion
Burn his heart
For the hand of the erotic goddess
Has never welcomed his flesh

He knows her voice
Her call
But to be delighted
By her touch
Or lips

Never!

So he partakes in the inevitable fantasy
On the couch alone
As medieval creatures, statues of night watch

On his couch
Half button lousy shirt

Identical
To his erotic attitude

He slips his hands inside his buttons

"A fleshly envelope"

To touch his chest,
Caressing himself gently
"Dialogue"
He says and impersonates
"Her"
As if she's there

"Oh lonely paladin
When's the last time you've been
Touched by a woman"

He replies
(Consciously knowing this woman knows anything
Will get him off)

"In two years"

Fondles his nipples
Like agitating peddles
Rubbing endlessly
To excruciating debauchery and sin

Rubbing his chest
And stomach
Endlessly
-believing she's there with him

O
Little boy
Get off now
And squirt streams of warm nectar

"Okay,
Please
Please
Please"

His solitude…
His fantasy

Just his hands
And mind

-calypso watches on

Running to the woods

I'll run
Like a curious child
Into unpredictable woods, cultivating,
Alluring odors

Louder than the phantasm of nature
Into deeper territory,
Where the drunken girls of Dionysus sleeps

I have rendered myself to you
Oh,
Rapture of woods

Whose trees hang over me
Like
Sinister parents protecting
My melancholic cloud

Provide a pillow for me…
And inside I can hopefully find a waterfall
Built by the hand of god
Just for me

Oh these despotic cries
I hear
Contemptible
Contemplating murder upon thy child

But I'll stand in front
Of the waterfall
Interpreting the language of the mysticism
From your roaring calls

Sprinkling on me
Answers to questions not yet arrived
I wish,
I can sleep here
Like the boys of Blake's vision

But since I'm subtle
And yearn for food
Ill might as well
Like some nymph…

Pick nuts
And berries
Or maybe bugs like john
And cry

Then go back to you
And make precious love
To the ground with my weary head
As if,
It were a woman

Bird II

A bird
Still with an earnest stare,
Looked as though
He was guarding the treasures of Eden

Head moving side to side
As if like a frantic pivot

To his left

What seem like black onyx,
Glistening in the morning sun

Ah I see
It is his fallen friend
Whose wings had delightful ambition
Shouting…

A protector of his friend
Who
Made his bed in the moist, morning grounds

Spiritual guardian!
Are you sad?
Hurt
Have you turned into a melancholic god like bird?

Joshua Victor

Thuds
He hear
Jumps
Leaves
"Him behind"

Because jeering footsteps
Dictated his destiny

Incantation

To...
I imagine, fantasize
I want so I conjure
To invisible masses
Whose vacant chairs
Shake by winds
And embellished by wood chimes

I know what's inside this hollow body
I know what I want
So paladin speaks…

The girl respects
The sage suggests
How painful the temptation I repress

I imagine I fantasize
I want
So,
I conjure

The blue one

In the realm
Where the quintessential sprouts
Out like blossoming trees whose black borders
Provide as silhouettes for velvet leaves

Drops dripping like,
The idea of solitude
One rolls off the leaf,
Slowly hitting the ground

Whose remnants
Splatters into dimensions of hysteria
So ill choose the blue one
That says
"For muse and ballads"

So I can enter and see
Aphrodite with her legs crossed
And her hands on her chin
Staring out of a window
Whose room is black as night
Looking as if she was contemplating
The philosophy of love
And looks at me
As if I'm a mate of fortune

Saying teasingly,

"Are you ready to take,
What you learned here
To tell and teach the others
In your so-called earth"

Glorious stains

Like rain,
Whose mystical urine stains the sidewalks,
As if to leave a mark
Like tigers vestige on a tree

Look at my stains
Whose adhesive nature
Is to show itself,
Where grey clouds hover about
Laughing
And pointing their rays
To embellish, my embarrassing terror

Comical,
To the mundane mindsets
Who the Egyptian demons
Has stripped them of their emotional attributes

Like Velcro
Snatched away from a melted corpse
Where the sun has burned

Poor fools,
Who looks to tyrannical, mediators of business
For direction
I see no use to care about you

But
It is the child yore
Whose pink blouse
Sprout
Off her young body
Like a cupcake

Embellished by pink ribbons
Embroidered around the frosting
And bulging eyes
Produce innocent marbles

Fixated on my stains
And doesn't laugh
But intrigued and point

"Oh child,
It'll be you I worship"

(Vulnerable confusion)

We all see the swinging pendulum
With the metal circular sphere

All of us fall into a trance
Whether by voices
Desires
Debauchery
Irrational acts out of frustration
Emotions or some fixed thing

We think about…
Monoideism

Myself
I get captured by teasing promises
And then indulge

I say
I sacrifice to burn

But I must say
To stay stubborn or empty
Is a transitional phase
To illuminating
Or haunting…
But anyways…

I must leave
To go get some more…
From…
I don't know

Black

Inside, turmoil
Who want to go against the rebuttal?
Black crystal
Precious gems

Never speaking
Always pretentious
Though it has melted
When I clench my fist of warm fervor

The panorama of the gem
To see infuriated flesh closing
In on it
Like steel walls of Cyclops

Dripping down my palms
Decorating my wrist,
Like black dripping ink
Or poison

Inside of rare
Reptilian creatures
Whose only instinct it is
To move its tail
Like unpredictable spasms

Right after it dies

Interpret
His slit eyes
The cunning phantasm
That we call pupils

Come

Come
Grip my hand tightly
As if
On a ride through pain and hell
Whose debauchery it is to torment gentle souls
Whose seeds provide flowers of righteous nectar,
Of blooming honey

Let us
Walk on thin lines
Dear child
Look down below to see
Gapping mouths
Inside tongue and breath of putrid odors
Remnants of bones and flesh
Decorate this house of death
Jagged teeth
Porcelain stained with blood

Hold my hand
Child

Let us journey
Through tortures
Where I pray for solace
Every time I breathe

Hesitating…?
(Know)
my friend will take care of us

Stampede of men
Whose cloaks signifies
The rider's wardrobe
Whose only wish is to see us
In the jungle of Ghana

Lost
Hopeless
And food for lions

Whose only wish
Is to grind on our flesh and bones
Splattering blood
As if heavy boots stomp on calm waters

Grinding
And the sound of bones snapping
Like the jaws of Siberian beast
Missing its target

Carcass
Dangling from wool ropes
Suspended in the fury of Normandy

So
Let me suggest
We smile and let our dark eyes embody
The fire of pandemonium

Bleeding
Without
Blinking

So that the beast
Who contemplates?
Sings songs

Cleverly distracted
By one unfathomable boldness
Who eventually swing its tail
And preponderant winds…

The last...

The last of the glowing sun
Whose ardent rays
Bleed red into the birth of dusk
Dying light screaming its last cry for anyone
To hear pity…

The light that for some reason illuminates dimly
Calling for the celestial moth
Whose vernacular
Can be translated
Into a dead flying bug whose haphazard wings
Flaps endlessly
In a fury
Trying to find its way or passage to the illumination

The rock trapping insects underneath
As if
Darkness is the light
Of scorpions who runs when the light is shown
Calm in the shadow of my body

A putrid stench of vestige
Of a carcass
Whose dead corpse cough
Yellow antiquity
Humid
Fowl
Disemboweled dreams scattered on brick yellow roads
Embroidered in it is pure gold

To see the end of the passage
You'll look at the beam of circular beauty
To which
This lazy man was cooked by the sun

Was this his destination?
Black…
No…

I shall walk this path to,
My skin melting rubber
So prevalent shown by loners and bohemians
Who embarks on trance like tortures,
Of searches
Are the stakes and prize

Our emblems

But the burning of our skins
Is the repetitive signal

I'll walk sluggish
Dying as I live
Oh
My knees they will be aching
My feet
Like the camels back whose
Passenger doesn't sweat under frigid suns

Inside
I see sand
Feel, internal Sahara

Joshua Victor

On this yellow road
I'll meet pain of steel

Just reach the radiating light!
Burning as I look
Who the other passenger tried
But failed
And now
His fate remains
In the mouths of vultures

Unknown worship

In an open corridor
Vacant
Stained
Dust grounds forgotten
Inhabitants
Discard waste and trash
Sitting there
Somewhat embellishing
The grotesque view

A black girl sitting sullen in disposition
Perched up against a brick wall
Hope,
Didn't plant seeds there

Her long face alluring
That stained my soul with pity
Wearing her dingy uniform
Stained in some parts

Sitting legs apart
As if tension and stress will relieve itself
Looked at me
As if saying,
"help me escape"

Dry crumbs
Rendering itself
Off her cracked lips

I couldn't look,
no more!

The baby burst into a sudden
Enchanting cry from unknown realms
Screaming as if pain revealed eternal adhesion

With a beret eating fresh apples
(dog?)
Usually would bark or defend
But his worship for this man is utter reverence

For he is the muse
The muse that sees

Eclipse

Articulate illuminating rays on the earth
Spilling yellow hostility upon our mother
The frolicking children playing,
The souls of melancholy submerge temporarily
Dubious minds…and pensiveness

Will their faces be embellished
In this bright day
Perfection for antiquity portraits
Foreshadows anyone to be influence by them

Frolicking
Frolicking
Frolicking

Eternal sun
Jubilant sways
And fun will be the plan

So tedious
Is the vibrant ebony of flowers,
Mocking the burning torches
That so easily get suppressed

When the glowing eye
Wants us to rage through
The
Day
Day
Day

Everybody running hysterically
Laughing
Lakes

Ponds
Pools
Rivers
Oceans
Beaches...occupied

By naked
Fleshly bodies
Water invading our pores
Breathing so hard
Unbounded joy arise in us

In the day
We feel
Express
No regrets
Unconscious minds
And our visons relentless
Makes itself known

Ahhh
Venus
Spread her legs
You holy whore

But we laugh, feel,
And succumb physically
To eternal day

Then from unknown whereabouts
From the left
Come creeping
Subtle
The veil
And omnipotent
Ominous blanket

Of death
Coming in
Squeezing the rays of our ideal
To the right
As if Hades were jealous
Squeezing orange rays
Until the darkness
Covered the earth
In brute animosity

The eclipse
Has devoid us
Into
Awe
Terror
Unbounded fear
Everything
Beguile
Like a dark magician
Playing sadistic tricks

Everything out
Gets bounded by leashes
Tie up these
Gay catapults

No more
Running

But silence
Stricken stiff
By the lightning of horror

My friends
This is the eclipse
You wasn't prepared

So festivities still being planned
Only by ghouls
And drunk merchants

Whose only wish
Is to bring about
Satan's crystal ball
And thrust it to the ground

Shattering it to smithereens
Releasing,
As if demons have time to play...

Frigid
Stiff
Daytime nymphs
Paralyzed

Suppression
Suppression

Stiff

Attention centered on darkness

The sun
The eclipse
Then us

Him
That
Then her

Ignore

Sitting with an adhesive physique
To a wooden chair
Only companion,
For a jeering night

Calmly looking at country bugs
Frolicking,
To their unseen domains
Normally your signal to leave

Death is here always sleeping
With one fixed debauchery of an eye open…
Telling you when preparation for departure,
But your emptiness ignore its sublimity

And your thoughts fixed on nostalgia
And nervous wishes
And hope…

What age
Will this become…

O holy one
With the scythe,
Quickly tickling my vison
Of daydreams

Joshua Victor

Naked bodies in the summer

The pungent summer
Of relentless body odors
Running and frolicking
With sinful ardor
Not yielding to the storms
Where unknown death surprises
Since eyes were not fixed
On the call of illuminating lightning bolts

That was ignored by pitiful bohemia
And it allocated to naked children swimming
In the lake

Caught red handed
Not knowing,
Now,
Four suspended bodies
Float
Like wooden debris
In
A
Desolate
Infested
Sea

Who was once blue,
With fish
Now
In the bellies of senile men

Jeering winds tells the small town
Rumors pass by
Like newspapers
Thrown from the young paupers hand

Bruised
Naked bodies
Radiating
On a summers eve

Joshua Victor

Now the excitement subsides

Mocking pecans
Falling off of spring trees
Dropping subtle on my vacant heading,
Murmuring emptiness
Repetition of unbothered peace

Sustained in the tip of my black eyelashes
At the point where it glows
Stands upright when the sun shine

Cautiously I use to utter excuses
Now yielding to boredom producing,
No responses to lamenting nervousness
Usually shaking the cryptic being

In my hollow tent fiercely

Now everything has reached its point
Of departure
For the hours of worship
Has now been masked
By rival phantoms

Whose only labor
Is to dig up treasure
Whose illuminating crystal jewels
Still sit

Intact
But
Was fondled
By a curious hand

The woman who beguiles

From persuading Shakespearean plays
Woman,
Who reigns in literature or television!

Naive
Docile
Yielding to straightforward demands

Daughters and predecessors
Make it easy
Only succumbing to benevolent smiles
Which I call the evil intents of eve

Snickering at the serpents hiss
Spontaneously woman portrayed in,
Drama
Books
Broadway
Acting

Is
The arbitrary
Of the act
Of which we would like to calculate

With the ebb
And flow
Of blood
Within the limp regions of our body

But woman
I see
Encountering mixed signals
Continuous flux

Once
Can be beguiled
By a certain beauty
Or trait they like

Suddenly
Turn that on its side
And evil turnover
Never pleasing

Gently
Feasible
We run mad over her

Who which is calm
In chaotic
Flux
Deliver
Us
From bondage
Of nostalgia of yesterday

No longer she brings worms
To her babies
Who strikingly
Dare to fetch for food
Before nursing

Cradling babies upset
Without any milk given
By prodigal mother

Not knowing
Unaware traits
Picked up by her
Who of course
Switches blouses
In the multitudes before
The stroke of eve

And dramas
Plays
Literature
Is a way she should be

As I nod my head
Cracked smile
Of repetitive confusion

Judgment from the cold

And,
What do you want me to say?

...why should I say that?
-well I will

For those who live in the mountains
Whose snowy peaks,
Melting like a white claw
Touching the orgiastic lava
Whose red and orange beat
Never gets illuminating...

Only when the phantasm of boredom
Creates obscure visons

You inhabitants,
Walk for miles,
Seeking the masses,
Hungry like frigid bohemians

Who have scruples,
Because the expense of sleep is a lot
For this mystic expedition

I say leave your homes
And cover all your possessions
With the snow,
You call a friend
Leave your children

The strongest among you
Will lead
And let your sway decide the way the marbles
Of glaze roll on the pivots

Bulging from curious heads
You will bring forth the treasure
To the sullen ones
Who worships cathedrals,
And four wheeled machines

You will tell them without blinking
As if Elijah was among you
Soothing...
Commanding...
Quietly
You will say...

"She was sleeping until we woke her
Now she is in a fury
And will decide the fate of y'all
She will look
As if examining your souls
To what you have produced"

Dagger

A dagger
No,
More like a steel javelin
Who which like a mosquito
Floats toward blood
Like a tormenting magnet

Whose only sin is not being able,
To stab with upmost debauchery
To see fresh blood
Maroon blood
Dripping
As if it calls out the owner's name

This dagger
Who has been made from the pit,
Of hell
Simmering, in a steaming pot

Ready to stab
As if it was taught that since birth
And
Since this stabbing seem eternal
And tumultuous
And will get in a despair disposition if
Its victim dies fast
(Oh fortunate ones)
I would say screaming
Because my breath allow me
To at least let out a painful cry

"Please dear dagger
Stab me where at least
I can have time,
Dreaming
About past fantasies
That were so vivid back when…
So,
That I can fantasize about a splendor
Of nostalgia"

Joshua Victor

Solace

That which I call solace
Is which I shall dwell in
As long as slaves on the moors
Moving slowly,
To slow down time
Which happens to be a delirium

In every case
In the eye of the storm
For my eerie nuisance
Beating in my chest

Taunting drums
From
The tribesman chant

And if by any means
The quintessential part of this bohemia
Is to endure the move
Whose fangs penetrate flesh,
Then let those
Who I call predecessors
And forebears
Speak from the graves
Of antiquity
With the advice of sages

Their beds relishes in mouths
Of maggots

In my domain

In my domain
The synchronizing knives
That cut through the air of night gently
Liquid instruments
Torrid rain

How you and your contemporary
(My heart)
Just are adhesive towards each other
Like an erotic bondage

I hope the marriage in which y'all plan
Goes well
But please don't invite your cousin

Whose taste in my heart
Is of tolerant disgust
Because you're involved

Never the less
Tied under cloaks of silence
In a church cathedral
Sitting on the pews of midnight
Murmuring verses of a child's plan
Renouncing
All festivities

How I ask ardently
To let the thunder
Show its presents
And lightning
Embellish
The pictorial
Works
Of Mary
And Jesus cradled in her arms

Lightning
I shall ask
Flash
Through these angelic pictures
And make them breathe

Oh how that
Romance
Will make
Your contemporary happy

Let us

Let us examine the dusk
For the muse
Is now scrutiny
Subdue your beast

In which has you under the spell
Of unconscious endeavors

I call upon men and women
Subordinates of the forests

Gentle children come forth
And examine dusk carefully
Some in our debauchery
Some in our nostalgia
Some our heads on walls

I as always
In a solemn stupor
(My causality, I know)

But now
Is time for all of us to tear off our rags
Our clothes

And let the dying sun
(Orange)
Radiate on these florescent bodies
-Since we will be naked examining
The dusk

Joshua Victor

Threshold

All of us are really wretches to begin with
Our beginning starts
At the door

Which the door knob
Is radiating sapphire

As if calling us
Luring us in
So alluring
Holy
Deviant as well

For we shall
Be forced to lie down
Our comfort
Our indigenous jewelry
Which is warm on our skin,

But now
What will permit,
Is running nerves
And a hastily heartbeat
Leaping out our diaphragm
As if a magnet
Is right in front of our naked chest

Our penis will shrivel up
And our intestines will turn,
Our dry mouths
Will know, no moisture

Remnants of our food
Will be our taste and tragedy
Sweating and contemplation
We are only at the threshold

What will our subterranean sun think?
To see the children of Eden sweating
Trying to confiscate our past comfort
For some type of closure and adhesive Band-Aid
That cannot be our chaperone

All of us looked deranged
And pulling out our hair
Screaming
Screeching
Gnawing the door
That we must enter
To reach our immortal gifts

Disregard,
The sound of the trumpet
Which is mute,
To the sound of nervous pandemonium

Dire pondering
Has crippled us
In a self-destructive bondage

Suddenly
Hesitant mouths
Murmur words of support

For which flames
Intercede on our behalf
Tempting us
To cry for our friends

But
Here we are alone at the threshold
And our claws which were once hands
Is already frightening us

For this immortal phantasm
Is coming from under the door,
Tired,
Of our hesitant input on our future

My only way through the day
Is to think about the immortal
Without being at the threshold

Fertile
Is the person
Who walks through,
Without comprehension or apprehension

Sustain the aroma,
Is first more intense
Than the smell
Of imagining,
Perfumes
From foul gardens
And fruits to ripe
And the green in the garden
Is forbidden green
Celestial green
The smell is unknown

Captured and suspended you'll feel
Within the first pass
Through the threshold
Sensible

Noetic
Cautious
But inclined
To the inevitable

Impetuous
Tempts us
Coughing tension
Full from the hunger
Food is not the nutrients…

For this power
Is immortal

Joshua Victor

Soft voice screams

Out of my chest is the plague
Which settles,
Subtle
Quiet
Simmering, never dying
Eternal pain
Which it is in
When it's not boiling
Or sustaining my fertile heart

Susceptible,
Are those whose claws cannot make noises
Scratching against metal
Screeching knives

The omnipotent
Which is so overwhelming,
My paladin is always,
Lurking
To see if I'm weak
Or tempted

The shadows are
No longer docile
They are now flesh
The scythe which I feared
Is now ideal

My grave
My comfort
Hammers
Hitting on nails
Dramatically
Or rest without ceasing

What is false?
Is eternal bliss
In this bliss

Temporary fertility
And jeering ecstasy
Has to be maintained
And its adhesion must not slip away
At any cost

I have missed out
I have missed out

Drowning
In a shallow ocean
Fishes and sharks
Move hastily away
From the squirming body

The seashore is ten feet away
But the outskirts are painful
The voices are dumb

His
Her
It…

All tragedy…!

Whisper

Silence
Silence

Let us enjoy this torment of burgeoning whispers
Whose seeds have taken roots,
Into its canvas

Stare
Stare

Into your eyes are ripe fruits bulging
Out its cave
To feel the air in which it's attracted
Don't blink, but strain those eyes

Into lightning flashes
That causes them to drip
And convulse in the strings of vessels
Open your palms slowly
Spontaneous
Feel the forbidden wind
Creeping under the door into your palms

Dry and soft
Permeable
Let your skin
Erupt with minions who huddle together
As if succumbing to cold

Breathe in the air that knocks
On your lips with its legs
And crawl into your mouth
Like a gentle spider

Feel baby
See baby
Touch
Hear baby
Taste the stale presence
Of the ghost
Whose only hope of life is to be,
On slime of saliva
And lie down
On his bed of tenderness
Wrapped up in bondage
As he meditates in the dark dream

No,
In the day

The sun from which
His hand made
Is calling us into eternity

-then
Eternity we shall fly

Joshua Victor

The paint that drains

The detailed premature sketches
That bleeds out of the artist hand
Is reminiscent of my life of torture
Brilliance
Succumbing to heavenly fatalities
Whose only meanings get interpret through dreams

A red sun dying
Illustrating the muse
Passion of ardor

Perhaps blue champagne rivers
Quietly floating downstream
Maybe the reflection of peculiar promises
Of peace and reflection

Dormant
And comfortable
A splatter of black
Dusk

Docile
Minute
Powerful provoking eternal gothic justice
The undead creep without temptation

Yellow,
Rays illuminating
On quiet penetrating mountains
Whose vastness and grandeur compliments
The splendor snowy caps

Mocking,
Is illumination,
Future
Death of prevalent fantasies

Regardless of what paintings
You make dear brother
As long as its liquid justices
Flood my porcelain tub

As long as the cork gets pulled
And the sick noise of color
Floats slowly down the drain
Making sick
Coughing
Noises
Leaving
Its remnants
And stains
My tub

Gone
Gone
Gone

I'm clean

Pollen finds him

Itching dandelions
Will sneeze its white remnants in the air
Like childish bubbles
Will hover and spread amongst the air

Each little one
Is designated to go to their landmarks
Whether it's on a human
A dog
A car
A house
Or simply on the other side of the field,
A puddle
Who knows?

Wise pollen seeking its home…
Nature,
The scavenger of the day
Hostile children frolicking
Screaming to see pollen

When will we learn?
That's it's the flowers of our predecessors
Whispering
Secrets of rapture
In the air gently whispering

Thousands
As if locust were the plague

Pharaoh screaming
And repenting

A ha
Off they go
Creating a haze of veils through the air...

But you'll see
As if fate had a mystic purpose for one
Floating
Distancing
Itself from the rest

(As if you can be a recluse?)
Floating
As if it was under the enchanting spell
Or a magnet held it by its genitals

Floats softly into this dark horizon

An abyss for demons
Into a cave
Follow if you dare

Floating,
Into the cave....

Purple cloaks on the ground
Shoes
Beret
A white undergarment...

"At last you found me dear friend
Is it my time to return,
To the world"?

Leave me

In a desperate panic
Leave me in my bohemia
Interpreting grey dull exterior
Claws of the raven

Whose pebbles
Mirrors
Black and luminous
Moves to and fro

For which light hits its majestic pupil
And reflects a path for the cryptic undead
Whose flesh leaks embarrassing maroon blood

In alleys you will hear blandly
Moans of echoes of women
Getting dug into
By well-endowed nymphs

Whose expression
Is September tortures,
And erotic deliriums
Panting both like restless dogs

Breaking glass
Screams…
Feet hit the puddles

Skipping boulders to desert crimes
Of Mojave
Or even Atlantis

The maracas shake
Steadily
Steadily
Shamanic drumming
Ecstasy prevails

Tears are the puddles
On the damp streets
From grief and pleasure
Gun shots echo through the air
Phantoms
Boomerangs

Decorate the solace of a loner
That's a passerby

Stumbling from drunken tricks
Grotesque,
Watchmen at the gates of a barbed wire house
Where Bacchus women of Dionysius
Provide as dark romantic statues
In front of the house

Apocalyptic panorama
Alleviates the premises
Of my boredom

For fountains burst out of hydrants
And loins

Drip
Until
You shake
And withdrawal
Quiver
Cum and your secreting fluids

Endlessly pours down your legs embarrassingly
Thick and white
Yellow
Flesh smells
From which it projects
Strong odor
Of your urethra
And your pungent fertility

Punctured…
Sated…
Girl…
Your mine…

Free…
But on a leash…
Dripping…

Come on baby

Excrete until you're dry
Down on me
Burst like a fountain of a rapture

Your seclusion
And reclusive
Your strict adhesion to
Anti-social bondage
Is now at walls
Of throbbing veins
And nerves

So burst
Be free
Of grief
And habitual,
Sustain closure
Censor…

You're my girl…
For you will drip as long as I
Puncture…

Gently burning,
Arch
Until the inside
Exposed

Hollow
Vacant
Dripping and constricting
Throbbing

Waiting for that man
In the outskirts
What
Will
You
Do

When he walks towards
You
Without fear
Eyes bulged
Sweat dripping
Drops of fire
From the dragons
Mouth

Bodies left for dead in a sauna
On your bed
Sheets
Dipped
In sexual moors

Tired
Panting
Thirsty

Help us…
Help us…

Entrenched and trapped
In
A
Eternal bondage
Of the kiss
Of Venus

I'm in the outskirts naked
In
Heat

Find me

I know you can't wait
Your heart aches
With the dull marble
Who never moves

And…
Hostile winds
Eternal dripping
Numbing
Quivering
Shaking
Righteous sinning

Your fertile woman
Your body belongs in my mouth
And your hair in my hand...

I'm in the outskirts
Find me...

Visions in the bedroom

Since these visions are at
The threshold
And balance on torturing lines
Let me suggest advice...

For the pink odor that will
Sweep under the door
And its frigid air
Will dump its fist on to your chest
And nipples

Which little bumps
Will form around
Like electric nerves
Penetrating flesh...

For I know what the cushions of her lips feel like,
A muse for which
Its potency of blood
Will be simmering under the skin

Which
Is an outlet of life escaping,
For expressing erogenous climates,
Whose weather is too putrid for clothes

Your behemoth,
Fantasies swim in your head
Like Eros,
Physical debris

So vivid will the next mans naked eye
See
And laugh

I know its ferocity
And its torture
Which stains like a burn,
From coal and moist adhesion

Fountains of tickles
Feeble joints pulsating
Weakened body,
Formless like a sensitive
Snake

Marriage of souls
Sharper than designs embroidered
In the goddess dress

Cool air for exposed skin
Debauchery and humid thickness
Suffocating under blankets
Dull walls closing in

Deserts of erotic cactus
Suspended and sustained
Tumultuous downpours
Of crawling worms

Leeches of pleasure
Excess of burgeoning heaths
Broken vertebrae
Tangible
And replace melancholy
Sunken into forbidden seas
Not yet discovered by divers

Drunken bats sucking
Sucking blood slowly
Invigorating ecstasy
Children of tantra

Realms
Of exposed indecency
Scenes of Paris
Broken headboard
Melting tombstones

Permanent in the hearts
Aching with blood
For futile chains
By excessive thuds

Chains
And padlocks
Cracked by devious brimstones
And calypso teeth grinding
And nibbling

Dogs of summer
Resting from fun
Scattered stains
Dubious aftershock

Earthquakes
Relying on damage for confirmation
Demons on the pillow cases
Odors of bodies
Climbing
To treacherous ceilings

Dancing with them who says
"The after shock
Is the beginning
Of the plague of storms"

Red drops
Sticking
Never removed

Diving in the throats
finding treasure
Planted by the hand of our ancestors
The tongues intertwine

A panner digging
And leaving
Remnants
Wormless diseases

Mountain lions roar
In heat with yellow eyes
Canons
And catapults

Starving
And ribs in an erosion
Diaphragm
Up
And
Down

Bodies tired
Sunken in cushions
Moans
And
Marriage

Tongues inside
Intertwine lips
Touch endless
Of expression
Of melancholic nostalgia

Have to be expressed
To reach the end
Climax...

For
Departure
Return to home
Sedated and weak

Frolicking
With trivial things
Never before
But smiling

Just to say
Wow
I guess

Where ill shine

Just as the sun
Illuminates
Its ardor behind a tree
Whispering secrets through the leaves

You get fondled and caressed
By transparent fingers that seem
To be its gentle preponderance

I to
Will shine
Not in my prime
Or full

But
In between beauteous people
Who whimper hymns,
Or sings songs

As they kick
Rocks along the road

Wounds without scabs

For your scab
That is a protecting roof
For your aching wound...

I would like to know
Who has punctured your silk skin?
That is the shadow
Of mere onyx

I understand that poison
Inside
Will never heal unless,
The subterranean
Gash get exposed to lamenting creatures

Whose skin is veils
Or tissues for their leaking nostrils

How many of us find scabs
Or scales
Along the roads?
To hurry and cover our wounds

Who which I should say
Heals faster when it is
Exposed
So that
The spirit
Of Hippocrates
Will be pleased
At our urgent
Cry to heal
Our vulnerable wounds

Medicine from the ghost czar

Cracked dry ground
Lightning there,
Have stolen water from this soil
Which is now a brown numbing plate
Ready to crumble in
Into the eternal core

A corpse
On the ground moving
Hesitantly holding on to life
As if the gift
Of golden diamonds melts in his
Burning hands

This body
From which maggots
Will be like a magnet
Is nothing but veins,
Pale flesh
And a silhouette for mere bone

Oh
You beautiful
Christmas tree

Red open sore
Like the opening of volcanoes
Oozing your red catastrophe
Like red ornaments
Placed there by Satan

Green veins splitting your body
Like a taunting
Tormenting maze
Jealously
Running down your body

Your finger nails
Cracking
Like yellow pearls
Shattered by illuminating light

Dull…
Breathing
Wheezing
As if a demon would repent

Murmuring
Your pitiful nostalgia
Crawling like a wounded reptile
But the Lethe is not here

Brother
So I would approach
Then tired of watching you suffer…

"I am
The ghost czar
Dear brother
Ill alleviate your pain
Render me your crystal garments"

-"Oh brother
Ghost czar tell me,
How will you cure
This suffering,
Quickly without pain"

"Like this…"

"Oooo
These beautiful crystal garments"

Joshua Victor

In the fields

I have lain down in the fields
Sated,
By desert dreams
Where the scarce whisper mocked
My phantasies

Sedated
This green moor
Where flowers have been deprived
And stripped
Burgeoning buds
Have ceased blossoming

And my bed
Aches my back
Like the sharp pillars of
Leviathan's fang

For my quintessential melancholy
Has found its essence
My
Black hollow eyes…

Daring,
But
Gently
Hoping
To find her
Scattered on the pedals
Of these limp roses
Who has curled into subterranean beds,

For which this bondage
Is comfortable
For it shelters its existence
Without bereaving

Obvious silhouettes that keep calling
Its name repeatedly
As if
"A woman's torture mocks her"

For I am sated
And I'm in a jubilee of fertile passions
That embarks on holy ravines
Thrown into the depths of the sea

For I have found exodus
Daydreaming
On this scattered field
For I will breathe
And slowly
Sleep

When will the heart freeze?

Since this pinching
From my scattered heart
Is of mites taken siege
Of fleshly prey
Has hindered
And without scruples
Found its way
Into the
Crows
Claw
Gripping
As
If
Frantic fishes
Yearning to be in the deep blue….

If my departure is sincere
Then I must shatter glass of champagne…

My maroon wine
Is the strongest of stenches,
And even more of the content and potency
For which it leaks

Like the ceiling,
Confronted by the
Tear drops
Of god

My black fountain,
Split by the nails,
Or fangs
Of wolves
Whose aggression
Shakes my spirit
Like
Raw meat of a fish

By the way
These Siberian wolves
Starved for three days…

For this subtle
Beating you hear
Faintly,
As if hiding from ears

Is not the fervor
But the dying
Of a heart
That capillaries
Hang
And
Cling to…

Like
An
Insect
Caught in the tormenting
Web
Of
The black widow

The crow is still feasting
Regardless
Of the infringement
And the cautious gluttony

So I would say as if,
I was a weary sage
Whispering to a
Child

"Down the road you'll
See a heart which is maroon
And blue
By itself by the gutters
Ready to burst…
Put a blanket over it
So that it's protected
From the cold that blows
Down from the Norwegian caves"

Sometimes as I...

Sometimes as I lie down
Where my innate vison is tickled
By the shapes it sees
On the bumpy ceiling…

My thoughts drip!
Pain, orgies
And forbidden fantasies
That can never get wrapped in a gift box…

My dear friend
Ill impale!
As if debauchery
Found an amorous grudge
Because
Of her sensitive vulnerable nature,

Infatuated with
The perversion of loneliness
Dripping thick drops of obscure white jobs
Escaping out of fleshly
Feminine chalice

From which this
Sphinx
Has punctured
And
Licked

Whispering
Disastrous fantasies in your ear
Tormenting your senses of
Adhesions to the walls of
Red rapture

My perversion is of a disdain
For which it dwells
In the tumults
Of the wounded Venus

My prisms from
Which your restless head
Will lie dormant
Will be transient…

That evanescence will be pure
But that purification that falls
Out the mouth of peter
Is reminiscent to the catastrophe
After you rest…

But
Oh dear sister
For this burning that takes place
When these eyes close
Are forbidden

And
Dark

Your body is too fragile
And soft for a rugged member
And your throat seems hollow
Like a holy well

And
My poison stains on mine
Will infect your throat
Choking off my saliva
And venom

While gripping your thighs
To make you screech

A hurt mammal
Caught in an alluring
Seducing trap

I am the man fiending
For your grace

Covering my Mojave
Jolted by the lightning
Of Ghana
That signals me to
Endlessly fondle
Your
Bond

With coerce hands
Paradoxically soft
As if this tenderness scares
Of aching nerves
Of electric phantoms

I'll leave you rotten
And hollow

Oh
Dear sister
Let me stop

Just thoughts
Just thoughts

"Now…
Yes…

I think you should get
Your mother a nice blouse
For her birthday"

Book II
Other mystics

Dear reader this is book II, at this point, I have lost sight of my poetic vision, comprehension and chronology is frivolous, quite trivial, here my beast reigns somewhat possessed by the sublime and the beast, which those will call the subconscious, but even if you was trying to find meaning I can't be a guide I myself, is an a maze in which it's called upon spontaneously. Sorry but it is really not my fault.

To write is casual, to express is an ideal, to create is worthy, but to suffer for the beast, to lose sleep for the beast, to free the beast to channel what you see, smell, feel, hear, and taste, to be a tent, a vessel for the eternal, an unknown language, in which the grandeur picks you as the poet, to tell its secrets…is incomprehensible

-J. Victor

Pondering scales

No one,
That I know has pondered scales

If so
A glimpse of an idea
Married in its martyred frailty

No one has pondered scales
Never rudimentary
I mean scales that burn in its brilliance
Where the obscure
"Black snow"
Is ashes
And
The archaic scales,
Whose vestigial, pilgrimage,
Is illuminating birds

Stabbing an axe
Or javelin in our liquid souls

That we hide in our tents
"Really prisons"
And the cries inside
And the jeering by the fluorescent light

All have a powerful stigma

But
None
That I know,
Has pondered scales

I see a jewel rolling on each fixed point
Where the exterior of its shape
Meets and congregates
At a fellowship

Deadly in an advance stage
Like
Hollow diseases, manifesting,

And its behemoth shine,
Strikes the core of the earth
And the delta creatures
Earth walkers
Come from the ground

Who in its rarity
We see every thousand years
Poke its head,
In curiosity

Asking with their eyes
"Who rattled my muse?"

I mean maybe here and there
But,

A couple of shockwaves
And a marriage of dreams
And at a creatures birth

Is a loud scream
Exiting a Nubian hollow world
Stolen from pleasure
In the back of a phantoms memory,

Captivating a break,
Now finger!
Touched on the back of the eye
Roll forward on the dilated pupil

And out mother's womb

But…
None…
None that pondered scales

Well decent
But not obtruding
In a temple of narcissist
Stomach giants on their backs

Where sprites and demons
Lay down their burdens
And the vessel hugging their talons,
Shake because the intercourse,
Has now been impregnated by a universe
Of crows

Stolen from the tundra's
Where the ancient king
Gets crowned
With jade and amethyst

Shining from their,

Desert
Swinging
Pendulums
Attracted to their roman knees

I pondered scales
But I don't know
Because…

I was born in a cloth
By the river
Where rushing miasma of water
Is my mother

And
A casual amphibian
Or reptile-
But

The lizard examined me
In my pupils
His feet on my hairless
Earth
Foreigner chest

"Yes maybe the water is your mother
But,
I'm not your father"

But
God at that time in my memory
So prevalent
Present
His omniscience
At that time poignant

But
It seem obscure
Because
I have to recollect
If I can

But right now,
I pondered scales

Where can my tombstone be laid?

Out there where the valley breathes
And the clouds echo
The flowers belch
My tombstone shall be laid

Here the hieroglyphs
Is encrypted
Under Helens wing
The smoke that you see…

Isn't circumcised
But in her nubile, birth
That nuance shall breathe prematurely

Don't fester the truth in sand
Nor pick lies from the fields
Of the barricades
Because my tombstone cannot be laid

First
Stifle the hammocks
On porcelain plates
And my myth caricatured
In Moroccan burnouses

That will be fine

But
My tombstone
Cannot be laid

Reptile your ember
Busy goes the queen bee
Haunting goes the fiends
Tickled your nerves of Nazareth

Pinch goes the buzzard
Now,
Now my tombstone cannot be laid

I or the ocean
Death or reside in the chambers
Of a cave
By St. Hermit

Under his trousers
Is a letter or words
That should be embroidered on my tombstone

And…
My grave right there,
By the soldier in a distant valley

Ah…
You found the place
Where my tombstone can be laid

I or he who renounce

It was only in my visceral
That I
Or shall say rather renouncing
That enduring Nymph within me

Found his way
Crossing sphere and road
Always jeering

So ever practical
To he who hides behind a dull renaissance

I
Who does this
So
Intricately

Finding crystal fossils
Rolling on its point
So steadily
Like the sun
Gleaming
On my neck

Oh precious eternity!

Find the pillars or salt
Vanquish at the circular eyes
That I trust when,
Hornets
Bees
And people,

Joshua Victor

Ponder this beguile
Present

It is I
Or should I renounce he,
That tires the evil doer
Whose maroon wound
Fosters craters

Ooze reptilian nightmare
Drip on the feet
Inside a hastily tundra

Oh my master
Sandal in a plethora
Count the pebbles on the shore,
By the Indian Ocean

Where those armor bearers
Go once again
Dancing
In spiral festivals

Catch unaware stares
Glares
And symmetrical
Communal
Mocking jesters

It is I
Or shall I say he
Who renounce

Tale of the boy and leviathan

Turned on its pale back
Is Leviathan
Crying the typhoon
Of hectic seas

I see
The waves
His lamenting bed
Licking his wounds

Never have I seen,
Blood
Diluted with crystal
Liquid,
In a rodent robust
Night sky

Where fangs of insects
And creatures
Pierce, peeled light,
In the sky

So heavily sated are the silhouettes
Whose black cloaks
Foster the ejaculated spectacle
The forefather of Diana

Craters in her aching pupil
Oh stop teasing leviathan
You night sun!

Wretched cries of humans
A fear not known
Panting and aiding leviathan

Inside is the book of lamentations
Worshipping their way
Through their pale, crisp,
Lips

Crawling are their,
Envious hands on its scaled
Diseased
Back

To nurture leviathan

Then the boy,
By his mother's lamp
Writing his thoughts
Through his fortune-telling eyes

Boring night

Synchronize ingredients
Fostered in a feast
Of loneliness,
Daydreaming

Leviathan
Leaks
He roars
The tears of wailing beast

Whose hindrance,
Is being numbered
Forceful like a nymph
By wanting ceaselessly,
To roam the buoyant
Eternal
Aching seas

His parents!
Is his thoughts
Of seer in the water
Beast of the awakened day!
Heaven away from the land

The creative boy daydreams…
Leviathan dies…
His soul in the hands of his mother

…precious boy…
No companion…
As he's weary…
Dips his liquid head,
In nocturnal dreams

Pregnant woman

Open
Sequence
Wild tundra's
Folly in a night gown

Where the aches of the terrain
Causes the pregnant woman to…
Upheaval
Her legs in a tumult of earthquake

Melt the furnace on a gentle bronze
My soul dull on the moors of mercury
Foster,
The tarnish in my spine

Disciple your willing spirit
Judas my aching bones
Dip cryptically
In the pregnant woman's stomach

Her hands
Jubilee
Fervor her pain
Her joints…
Nauseated, new birth

A sickness before a new kingdom
Temptation before a new ministry
The earth shakes,
Because of forbidden royalty
Let it rain roses!

Inscribed are murals and maroon cloaks
Being tickled
From below
Of demonic tongues

Spring
Jeering is the soil
Telling us to relay the message
Back to her

The pregnant woman
Her arms intertwine
Wretched bewilderment

Hades armor bearers
In the branches
Where their talons
Grip the branches

Like protected
Prude children
Singing
Eternity snatched

The leaves so docile in the patriarch
These cretins absorbed
The pregnant lady's tumult

In their eyes
Marble
Crystal
Spheres
Haunting her tortured spirit

Laughing,

"Pregnant woman"
They say
Pain is your vagabond
So adhesive your first child
-since womanhood

Birth a new world
Sorrow and jolly enchanted
By eyes peeking
At you
Behind tents
Wondering your dilemma

Ankles
Of her
Stated
Feeble
Swollen

Her hair
Molten
Disastrous zephyrs

(Who by the way blows
During deserts and famine,
Where water is scarce like African sapphire
In the open country)

Pregnant woman
The panorama
Scenery

Worshipped
Dark mystical rapture
Deacons as vultures
Windstorms of peter
Cries of Sodom
Zephyrs of condemnation
Moon of awkward instincts
Jeer
Creature
Pungent eyes
Cries and screams…desert worship

The baby…fruition
A dream…solace
So haunting
Peace when the dream
Is eternal

Let us now worship
Our wounds
The sweat,
Now are blankets
Chirps
Water
Oasis

The child points and says
Without anyone understanding
What pain?
What departure?

Mystic I

To see a ravens claw,
Is as precious as the heart
Being drowned in a black oasis
My lightning striking the grass
Serves as a better
Mirror
Who's to say those scales
Once leather
And reflected gaily
Is now shed skin

The raven's claw
The lightning
Scales…
All appreciated
By the optical
The sound of water
Into the back of a majestic whale,
Mounted on a rock of gold
Tedious gem
A pillow for my salty head
Subdued
Treasures
Rivers of violet
Forest of kingdoms
Deserts of animals
Silhouettes of butterflies

Cuts deeper
Than the lumberjacks knives
To a core
You're envious of,
My leaking flesh
Worse by night
Coughing up lizards
Or steel bread

Mystic II

The sea and the Neanderthal
Peaks or plateaus
The hint or mystic clue
Is subdued intricately
The state of searched patterns tick clockwise
At three

Penalty of default
Valley or bridge
My parallel has ceased
To scream relish

Soft or minute
Dubious or temperamental
My bird has clumsily
Fly limpid

Yeast or basket
Slave or willed
This yellow catastrophe
Screams dead banquets

Colleague or forest
Azure and steeds
My hollow prism
Still lies in ridge

Solemn and savored
Drought or frost
This dubious nymph
Screams
Her bloody hideous

Feast and famine
Cry screeching cliffs
All the time
Spun under a current
Hidden in the eyes
Of a jewel

Maker or destroys
Clouds and dung
This fertilizer
Begs heat

Relish and flamboyant
Caught in the stencil
Which was sowed
By a web

A seer jubilant,
Breaks and splits his apple
And tempting to eat bare
No napkins for the degree of urge

Turbulent or fierce
Storm of collard
Always hinders
Vestige sleep

Awaken and doomed
Soft and still
Detach these stars
From the myth and meanings
Drool dogs
In your heat
Of putrid moisture
Solid festive

Celebrated on a minute basis
Spins boisterous dances
And green vernacular
By cooked blades
Blinded green
On uneasy horizons

Still,
We throw our thrash
On top of orchard hill
Dandelion and decay
Sloth for a frenzied mist
Fog on the couch
Tormented house
Dew on our tables
Outlets corroding
The roots
Rotten
Seeds
Sullied sullen genes tortured
Continuous crash,
So baffled
And mocked
By our fingernails
Bitten by our ancestors
And fossils by our kidneys
Scratched futile,

Ardor in palm
Thrust the door to fellow our faces
Envying a desolate image
Reflected on our enemy
Traps
Glass
Leather
Transparent
Phantom on our sink
Drip blood

Here I must say

Here I must say
This lunar night
I whispered chills
Sustained in a bowl
Of food whose triangular urns
Was burning sulfur
More than a brand

I can go personally
To naïve stars wondering
So intricately
By a fountain of ordinance
No adhesion,
No mere bondage can separate my soul
In a desert or realms

I once opened the door
Perpendicular forests
In a castle of vestige
Apes of drama
And a core of molten lava
Dripping icing
On top of a frozen steel cake

This iron!
More miraculous than glory
This tempest
Higher than the medieval building
Castle in a tyranny
Flowers in the sea
Dirt or moist land
Moors on the bloody bondage

Joshua Victor

Scoundrels
And festive drugs
Colors is an astute
Pyramid
My moth has
In his celestial path
Better cotton
No unused fabric
Drenched in
Blood
Clothes
Or
Fur

Fragments of the still
Feeble and your grind
Frolicking and desirable
Forced and freely hostage
Slave in my mind
Finding penguins to dance to your bohemia

I came to bring
Here…
I must say
My odor
And notch batch
Or warren

I have entered
And exited on that ground
Where I fell asleep

Painful departure

Since she has found her treasure
A panner graciously wails for her paladin
I myself beguiled
Frolicking like a child

Awaiting
Delightful treats
Which she has wrapped

Is now,
But a dream!

The satire thrust
Upon me
Is of molten
Burning its way
Through the luminous hole
In which its seeps and boils
In my heart

The symptoms
Of a frailty
Gentle heart!

How normal it is
To hold it in

Satan!
That leader of demons
Laughs
As if to say:

"Your woman …
Let's see what she'll
Do next"

Have stolen the few berries
In which the seed cultivated
Now since her paladin
Has swept his mistress
Off her feet-

…I guess
It's time for me to gather
What I have left
And kick dust with the stare of indulgence
As I head on treading
The grounds
Whose companionship
Never left my aching feet…

Greeting

Sediments of grey cathedrals
Whose ominous black sediments
Crumble from these ancient bricks
Gets picked up from my hand

Who's to say gallantly
I arrived with a sway
In which I evoke
Pride!

These shadows who never breathes
But mobility shatters this barrier
In which I call solitude

For a recluse who sees nothing
But the sound of cry's,
Screeching,
Wings
Engaging
In intercourse
Fondling a vibration
In which it emits like a wave
Mumbling her existence
Creatures and skylarks
Insects
Of the open cave

But this fertility
In which like a trance
Induces
Caught me elated

Jolting phantasm
Has told me
Shun the outside
But of no hostile barrier

All pandemonium crumbles
A way when a voice greets me
From the canvas
In which the multitudes share

This is what it calls for

And
Since the fever has subsided
In the chills
Which is so riveting
From the iceberg
That once boils,

Let this plague
In which the heat
Melts my panorama
Of the synthesis
Which is extracted,
From eyes
Which are too big and fixed,
That it encircles a curious
But represses
Lashing-out,

I will have to say
As if the heartache will allow
Take the feces in which
You deposited
Throw it in the sewer

Where the creatures
Lie in waiting
For its food

Mystic III

Out beyond the threshold
In which you betrayed
I
Like the golden reef,

Swing from branches
Like omnipotent children
Whose faith
Juxtapose
Suspension

Never my blood flows
As in a hour glass
Where frolicking is more measured
Than time

I yield when I see the skylarks
Eyes pivot
As if curiousity is the emblem
Of time

For when this occurs
Who can capture
The steel in which
It bends like elastic

Springing spontaneous
Desire
Which,
Repressed
Or actively uncontrolled
Marks the distinction
Between righteous and wicked

Mystic IV

On these premises
I will welcome you to the dripping threshold
Who liquid splatters
Like yellow robust drops of nectar
Staining your shirt
Burning holes like sensuous lava

Signaling to you to banish
The tavern
In which you take shelter
And roam freely on the outskirts
Of Norway

For where phantoms,
Not demons
Follow close by like,
Intentional shadows
Whose owner mocks the sidewalks
Of midnight as he reigns

Finding his shattered crown
In which the hostile wind
Fondled
And
Bewitched

Into an tedious maze
Where golden keys
Signals
Or checkpoints

Joshua Victor

I have seen the preponderant nymphs
Who laughs
While sustaining
Reality in a glass cup

Where burgeoning spirits
Tempts the silhouettes
Of a courageous flower,
Who was once a seed in a farmer's hand

Mystic V

These crystal jewels
Whose circular silhouettes
Moves temptingly in the sunlight
Is made up of a burning water
That castrates itself on the ax
That comes down with judgment

Ceaselessly this burning, which
Permeates my eyes
Ironically
When left out its home
Is frigid cold rolling
Over the bridge of my nose

Cool, or lukewarm

I wonder if the boulder that lies
At those barracks,
Have a foothold
In the hollow vastness
That seems transparent

I just wonder does the remnants
Or sediments
Gets pushed into these drops,
Which is like rain from the clouds,
Of Dionysus
In a lonesome winter…

Never the less
I am inside with…
These scruples have hindered
The…

Ah god,
I will end it here

Sonnet of a wilting flower

By the foundation of my heart,
Whose water was springing gaiety,
Of omnipotence
Unlimited tundra,

I saw slouching,
As if weighed down by the burdens of a widow

A wilted flower

"Oh muse"
He whispers,

Frightened
The curious nerves,
Whose electricity was of lightning

Only spotted by the naked eye
I positioned myself by it
As if
Not to look like a strange man,
Whose delusions
Overwhelmed his panorama

"Dear flower you speak to I"

"Yes I do,
For I know who to call in
I know the feasting of midnight,
Who simmers in the heart of a sated,
Bohemian,
Whose circular onyx is bred in dungeons of ecstasy

But dear muse hear me..."

"I have a burden of solitude myself
Winter strikes me like,
Plagues of Europe
Pain for which,
Is a nymph
Or eternal captivity

I have tried to hang myself
With the pedals I have
But few,
My friend I possess

The wind I call to
As if,
It would respond to a wilting flower
On his last leg
Of fertile chastity

I have searched for the marble
That seems so transient
That orange flame,
That falls out of the blue skies,

That burning
Which my green erects
Like a voluptuous woman
Who excites the man in seclusion,
Ever freely giving herself to him

But
This backstabbing sun
Who resides in a subterrean bed,
Glimmers faintly in this putrid weather

Oh muse
I know no language of time
But tell me,
How long until Spring?

…
"25 days"

"Are you mocking me,
With such, wicked longevity
That you sullenly say as if it
Were good

Oh muse,
I must apologize
It's just deaths stench
Is of trash in a barricade or corridor for days

In which hours
Are mesmerized by its own presence
So its position move slowly
Just to taunt me

…and these heathens
Frolicking all around
As if spring is eternal

But…
Hmm
Muse
I see winter in your eyes to…

Are you wilting to
Wilting slowly away
Have these menaces,
Snatched your pedals

And
Have given you
Arms instead,

Come now,
Let us wilt away together…

And
By spring we will rise
As if debauchery and death
Is surprise by this…

Resurrection
And torture
To the bereaving children,
Who has caused your winter…

But as of now
We will
Will wilt
Suffer
And
Die

Mystic landscapes

So gently,
Let there be landscapes
In your carved soul
Devoured by my,
Forceful eyes

Let the mongoose drip from every edge of your skin
Foil burning
On your sediment of a back

Jubilee bitten in your crucifix
Stabbing dandelions in your retina
Clinch your bells
Stoically capture ghost in shells
Frolicked in a cage
Torturing red robins

Free the hills,
Sphinx impregnated in Siberia
Torn,
Is the duplicate Nigeria
Found reaping embellishment

Wonder the claws of a raven,

Feet in rugged terrain
Hindrance the impotent castle
Frigid in Otranto,
Knight my chivalry
Cautious my steed
Blood awakened nice moors

Joshua Victor

Stench in your cry
Fear the wolves,
Caught in a web
Impressing the mocked scoundrel

Festered in its miasma
Moreover is the rotten nest
Food to the
"Little ones"
Whose wings are comic,
Joke to the air
Stampede
Burning
Found in a shell

Scream Herod
Scream Pontius

My call is here bleeding my angel
Drench my curtain
Stain my precious roots
Penetrate the clustered soil
With your vines

Seed and my tree forever
Given birth to
Meling

I'm empty
For the tomb
Weary at best
Whipped with coals
Tickling my perplexed feet

Find the girl,
Who goes Panama in her maze,
Scorched on her back
Is hanging skin

Mere fossils
For pebbles,
Once running through the hands
Like sensual granules
Of sand
Of war
And
Suffers
Of archaic adventure
Hidden secrets
From the village leaders
Incognito
Breathing in fumes of whales
And desert cocoons
Giving birth to ointments
And
Rotten pillows too hard for a sleeping head
Its giant body
Suspended in nebula
Pointing
To its lost home

My demon
Or
My angel

Room or cave

Enter the room,
My child
Seething
On the walls
Are pupils

These are mirrors to the host
Crystal wind,
Blowing
Fear awakens
Nerves running

Dimensions,
Found in your state of vulnerability
Your ego
Your shield
You obey...

The stoic!
Are you righteous to go stoically?

...he laughs at your emeralds
Illuminate,
The caves

Gargoyles huddle together
Choking
Eating
Mocking
Laughing...

Naked is their flesh
Phoenix burning their eyes
Soulless
Devoured are their pupils
(red rivers, mildly thin, suppressed under the brown archaic flesh)

Dripping blood from their fangs
And talons
The desire of their path is to pulsate
Oozing
Wicked,
Dripping from the corners of their mouths

Maroon is their worship
Sacraments on their lips

Menacing at their guest
You
You are their guest

Enchanted
Abominated
Bacchus
And Maenads
But worse

Frenzied through
Sensualism and murder
Abysmal carnivore
Under the spell of rapture

They circle
As if like mystical
Initiation
They dance around you…

And
The smell of the corpse,
Insatiable carcass
Objective
Projected towards your nostrils

Their genitals
Flange
Gyrating,
To the east and west of the continents

Smell of the ancient,
Syrups and humid venom
Odors of the flesh
Permeating,
Seeping

Thawing out like frozen meat

Like a pendulum
Or
Hypnotize in fear

Gripping their neighbors hand
Closing
In on your personal aura

Invading your innocence

They dance in circles
Faster
Oh dizzy
Wrath

The mirrors
Blink,

Wretched cries

And
A gargoyle
Whisper
Leaning as if,
An augury
Before a bewildered feast

"Girl……
You better…

GET OUT

Joshua Victor

Mystic identity

I am a native
I am an inhabitant
I am the indigenous
I belong…

Now,
You, green vernacular
Ordained in Venus
Do not in your storm,
Speak thunder in your spoiled nest

I must divorce
My lamenting bride
Her bayonet,
Just like the black widows web
Caught an insect on its back

Wondering,
Smelling that antique smell
That stalked Adam and will
Hinder that last man

I am alone
Solemn,
Sullen
Somber
Romantic

I am vestige,
Or in a monotonous pillar
By an ogre with his renaissance of wardrobe
Saying his prayers in ill repute
Resenting
Petition to the cathedral
In a night where those dewy mountains,
In its grandeur
Cries the sublime exodus

I in my traffic
Frolicked and spirit…
Teased…
This by
Myself
I express

To the scoundrels

To all the scoundrels
In black
Whose,
Gory
Reluctant
Cauldron of melancholy

I have come with my crown
Not embellished by gold and onyx
Nor in sapphire or ruby

But

In gray lines
Lines that forecast,
Avenues
That jubilant fervor
That beast whose fangs,
Is always seen in the crystal ball
By that entrenched gypsy

Who's to say we put our trust
In a woman
With antique hands
Pale,
Grey sullen skin

Purple
Maroon
Blood
Penetrating
Her erected skin
Of
Death

Feeble hands
Gripping
A clear Neptune
Spinning our tumult
Of child,
Shaking
Our pupils
In a soaked desert,
In a melancholy oasis

Our vulnerability
Entrusted with her

Oh you sacred vow
Oh you sacred will,
Given to a child

Death taunting

Who was the psalmist?
Was it David?

You cried
Treachery
When friends like,
Red envelopes
Who come and go
Like messages

My stanza
This stanza
Is my divorce
So welcome me home
Like the son drenched in foreign odors
And whose stomach,
Like a home
Protects the envious mud and feces,
Which was stolen from hungry pigs

Tad poles and frogs

-Take heed

Look,
There in the streaming river,
The silver silhouettes
That ever-increasing,
Collage of liquid steel,

Beating its omen,
Deadly to the crows eyes
An answer which was reluctant,
At first

But
Now with shudder,
And jumps on the wings of the moth
Hastily flying…

Which the frog,
In his sullen daydreams,
Creates time and space

Easy
Synchronizing
Chimes of the insects,
Tadpoles
Tumult and courageous bellies

Never in their sustained millennium
Have I seen oasis,
Clustered with a scattered shell

No
In this shell was a land of promises
Knick knack,
The boots of their biographies
Spill its molten influence
In the stream

But
Half heartily,
The ducks and their young
Drown their ardor
Which hides in the black panthers eyes,
Secluded yellow and his pupil,
Like a knife cutting its boomerang through

In the utensil of the shaman
Rain dancing
Whose eyes like seldom

Revered
Catches the stove of the drink
Of intolerable pain

I have yet to see with naked
Eyes
Clothe in precious red veins
Rubies of insomnia
Tell my picture or untold mountain

In which like the clouds obscure peaks
Aching and grabbing Zeus,
At his ankle

Screaming, like bolts
I will strike the ground
Spontaneous

And
I…
Crouched down tickled by what this frog,
Just whispered

Mystic

Mother!
The patriot,
Like a vessel through Golgotha
Is death

But to condemn that hour hand
Is futile
Because my soul,
Trapped in a frenzied cage

Those claws like igloos cools my nerves
Painfully
Hence the echo carries,
Until the tomb is barren

Shaking

So your heart is not jumping
But itching
Parasites so righteous,
Suck your maroon manure
And that fertilizer,
That pricks worlds one by one
Those blades like apartheid
Separated
Have no idea that Venus in her lovely dress
Was naked by summers midnight

So
If those naïve bells
Which hangs
Bumps like the masochist and testes
Always drool

Well the dog in his ponder
Will say
It is not the bone from which I don't have
By the jubilant architecture
Missing in the fossil

So when I steadily and humbly,
Insert my frolicked finger,
A child's tongue inside the quiet rivers of Lebanon,
I am not disturbing fishes (so putrid on humid nights)

But
Rather waiting for Poseidon
No the gargoyle
And aqua

No
But her
Who if be,
Put in language
Resembles mad Ophelia

But her skin
Like craters
Dehydrated and jealous
Crumbs of scab mount on her face

It is
Because the scrotum in which like porcupine
Arise when disturbed
Will let me in the wilderness
And its natives

Nor the stoic
And fruitful
Men in the Mediterranean
Who by the way said their prayers

On their peak knees like rustic shovels
Humid handle by anxious panners
Go woo in the ground

Make impressions of that patriot
In Golgotha
Jesus?

So to say their prayers
Or sacrileges scream
Or the dim light sun
Teasing the distant mountain
And
The constellations playing
Our ancestors
Those winds which like flesh
Physically tickles,
By its aggression
Similar like slaves running
With broken chains

Iron from it melted into my onyx ring
Then our mother…

Mother,
Patriot
But who would tell about
The cave men in the Mediterranean
Burying his corpse to hades that happens,
To knock on the roof of our houses

The divorce

Now you are free to roam
With the brilliance of the mystic expedition
We can now divorce ourselves
The black widow kills her husband

Mutilated and abandoned
Scratching,
Swinging
There go the scored legs
Motionless

Like the frolicking can
Whose stencil is poignant,
And dared
On the edge of a motherless gutter
So steadily

The divorce is gut wrenching
Underestimated
Novice,
Sepulcher and seraphim's

Nearly
Teasing
Memories
So unsure

In the grave
Bending
Tortures
Or brail
Who knows?
Who knows?

Joshua Victor

My sullen night

Now,
Currents,
Quiet creases
Bowls of grey liquid
Cautious and tedium
Gently ill ebb and flow
Bells on a plateau
Stir naïve spirits
In a witches awakening

Cave and still
Flow easily down the devoured stream
Choking off of coals and cloaks
Drowned in boisterous angles
Prisms in my catastrophe
Elm and chocolate abandonments
Foolish nymphs
Cocktails and desert syrups
Whose serum is so sullen,
On a plank of cold wood

Dreary my easy
Simple that trough
Foretell my foreshadow
In your eloquent horizon

Cast your web on pricked skin
Tickled and angered skin
Frolicked in a gelatin

My hypnosis subdued
Fill free to grab my cloud
On a tilted earth
Mounted in a cauliflower
My mother cooked

My cauldron repressed
Repressed what?
Jubilant natives
Dancing to embellished music
Embroidered by sullen tombs
Fixed or broken tunes

Supposed my falcon
Has in a clustered shell
A scurried nest
Harvesting a harnessed
Binge
Whose mask bleeds through seams,
Like dry clay walls broken down
By metal drops of rain
Horrid
Torrid
Condensing clouds
Hugging my aching head

I'll show this tangible booze
Bubbling…
Breathe my gallant phantom
Still my novice
Muse
Ill scatter and bow for my sullen
My sullen hooks

Joshua Victor

If the hiccups go sullen then what will bring the noise

This stanza will suggest
This stanza will project
This stanza will…

Never mind the sullen hiccups
Who subdue itself,
In your belly of tumult
Who like wine in glass
Hugs a thick vestigial liquid,
Around those toast intestines

Never have I said with such fervor
Belch and scream
For this,
Pandemonium teases

No
It caresses
Fur on its hindrance touching
Pale skin

Softer than,
Condensing clouds
Drown in your acid
If you do not belch
Project your empire

Hurry the wise man
Whose crow,
Go lurking
In your night

Face this mischievous
Not with pity
Piety
But with sound
That echoes like god
In a tumult of seashells

Broken impotence
We all decide
In your shattered melancholy

Now this ignorance is like,
Bereaving
Dreary
Moth to tears

Which like moles,
Dried liquid are adhesive to its bitter wings
Like
Flesh and blood
Capillary in an insect

Portrayed in a raisin
So my call
Which saved you in your amazon,
Is not a tempting gesture…

Than what you and your procurements
Recedes
Than under the third layer of putrid wings
That the raven hides but the sun exploit
(Oh by the way with its bloody nature
And its gore nothing can run from it)
So put it there under that birds emblem

So rustic and spontaneous
Like a lighted
Dull
Treasure made not of gold but,
Jade
In which the encrypted words are like,
Hieroglyphics
And jade embellished on its silhouettes
Edges,

So
What
I'm
Really
Saying
Is,

It is also the tombstone of the phoenix
Dress not in the boisterous orange and red
Who envies that intertwined engagement,
Not yet vertical
Nor horizontal as veteran spouses
Than any couple so sacred in their
Closure

Hidden in a black crystal lake
Like gems of onyx not yet fondled
I'm saying not like the glint,
In a child's eye,
When boredom destroys the frolicking and fun

But more like,
The glint in the senile eyes
When the memories of joy and youth
Ejaculate in a present oblivion

Who hugs his joints,
Like a caterpillars feet on rocky
Erected
Tree trunks

Auguries of caution

Is it our turn,
To flip those angelic toads on their backs
Is it our turn to clean the lily pods?
Are we righteous to judge the octopus?

Tell Dionysius that the orgiastic wine,
Is subdued, because now we marvel at his laurels
Tell Aphrodite and Venus that envy reigns

Now on your anecdote
Is a dubious tyrant whose throne,
Just like the gold in dirt,
Is embroidered on our wooden floors

The peasants pick up their pandemonium
The moon teases us in its crescent
Awaken the moth
From its sleep
It goes hiding in the day wrapped in its nectar

The green council
Parliament and senator
And your majesty drools brown rheum

Filth of the bats whose eyelids,
Like drenched blankets
Hides
Its worried pupil

Then the marble hindered in its feet is the spider web
That
Like your secular part,
Hits my ribs and vertebrae

What spider?

In all of your clutter
This mountain of stanza
Ties my feet like Hecate in the pits of hell
Directing black behemoth goats to read her words
Of worship…

Pay attention reader to the language of mystics
The augury of caution:
        In your rectangular sphinx
        Where the cats both feeble
        Bend like the bridges in Europe
        The orange eyes and those sullied bags
        Or baskets
        Closes at dusk
        Finger pressed
        And fondled by her hair
        Amorous are the Spanish traditions
        When will the moth sit on my shoulder,
        In its brilliance as I play the harp
        How long must the creole fish of the Atlantic
        Hold his breath, till Hades in its slumber
        So reluctant, and in its sloth free the souls of men
        Whose sin penetrates like molten rock
        Which was last seen being brought into being
        At Lebanon
        When came the dawn and your cataracts
        Suspect the oath between lightning and rodents
        Adultery inside it,

Debauchery
Make its way to the Netherlands
The manor is not being seen with the ox
No,
That in itself is too righteous
But,
The fox cut its claw on the bark
Because in his anxious feeling
He thought you left him food
But,
Your native leaders
Your scotch,
Oriental rugs
Brought you slumber back to Damascus
And your astute pedigrees
Now burns in acid,
Where Dionysius laurel was last seen
And like the rendering of love
Wasn't enough punishment
For aching Venus
She in her melancholy praise
And her mud tears of sonnets
Said:
"No it is not envy that peaks and
Brings my futility, but it's the evolution,
Of disintegration, the memories of a stained glass
Never remembering the dirt, once it's clean,
Free from dull wisdom,
Now illuminating some other brilliance and,
Ill refutable fluorescence"

Obscure vision

This is what I found,
Freezing in the caves of Greenland

Were our ancestors,
Wounded faces
Fangs
Vestige armor embellishing

Knights in the night guarding the dead
Scared on their post

From the desolate rampart stood…
The nymph

And I heard the tombs scream
Crying like a baby
Without food
This I couldn't bare

My blanket was in a tumult of infatuation
My body mere inspiration
As muse
To the tempting gates of Fuseli

Storms
Enchanted
Rapture in my spleen
Desert in my lung

I captured the panoramic view
Scenic
In sublimity

The creole descendants
Suppose they were…condemned

So the misunderstood wailing,
Is now fruition
Of the stand
Stock,
And now the yards are yielding

Busy is not the carpenter
But the morgue
That coughs up dead bodies hogtied
By sin

Princess

Wooden sphinx
Epic
How beautiful
Radiant in your prestige…

Are your fangs

Empress silver jade
What rubies
Illuminates your crown

Never has my race
Every busied itself
With your vermillion

Outspoken on our windows are,
The rays of winged crickets
Eyes,
Trapping spades in a diamond

Anchors in my wedge
Shakes and rattle in your pilgrimage
Truth finds
Claw skinning the flesh
Hiding in a crystal shade

Departure leviathan
Hidden on its chain
Your glossy scales
Of armor doesn't scare me any more

...than those fishes you swallowed
Being seen alive
Again...

No laments for me
Just evolved
Species
Shedding the primacy of peters antics

A coat embellished
By shapes and holes
Clues
Found broken
Hints the calluses
Washed over
From above

Bye
Princess

Stutter

Caress
Broken arrow
Do your ghost dance
Your prayers in paint
Words of my heart burns
Clustered in a extroverted seashell
Are puzzles and ridges

Bride
In her bouquet of dresses
Fondled desolate before the bridegroom
Reeking havoc or stencil

I am a walker
Mumbling talker
(Stutter buster)

Fragments drowned in bells
Pillow heaven
Deserted oasis
Each trough in the semen
Is characters or beams

When will this monster
Stop bragging
When will this monster
Stop dragging

Peeps and nuances
Everyone tell a folklore
God-like candles
Dripping amorous wax

Duly and bereaving
Swaying hips
I can always choose your moniker,
On the beach

Cool guy
Drenched in sweat
Labor in his palm
Turmoil and molten lava
Being refined
In the iron of our,
Sublime

Awe inspiring statues

Cryptic is its history
Cryptic is the shell…
Stoically

Release on Christmas Eve

Now this forbidden,
Stakes and swords
In a unduly
Rock,
King Arthur victor
Hero…

Solemn inside this needle
Riding down this bevel
Is a scarecrow,
Who shuns
But ill hesitate,
The moon,
In your lunatic
Pompous in your celebration

Now the raven whispers
While dripping from its beaks
Answers,
Jealously,
Swings its wing
Blinded by the airborne debris

Sensations and catastrophes
Button in a tin can
Color to the rim
Drip cool jade
As a undressed spoon,
Put to these lips
Food of bowel and foul

Joshua Victor

No more I grind
With the lake
Whose ice surface,
Stains
Busy by the pardon fish,
Swimming in the deep

Drooling,
Deserts
Crystal and poignant steeds
Upheaval cannot,
Drown my meniscus

Covered
Tugged
Seclude
Hidden in a ogres hug
Fountain of remnants

Jolly is a few hours
But who can,
Like a vacuum
Suck the desires,
Of flowerbeds,
Before the hibernation…

Quicker than the ghost,
Fleeing from the glint,
Seen in our humans eye

I know not sacrilege
Or maybe subjective
But the hour glass,
Pours to and fro
Paused,
For a dawn to create

Conjure the magician,
But not the horse
Whose midnight shadow
And architecture,
Burying its face
And
The dubious horseman,
Hindered by the sparkling gem
In the concrete

Joshua Victor

Humans and other kingdoms

Faintly
Hollow or maybe an echo
Ponder!
Oh,
African maracas

My body gyrates in my dreams
Sweating a tumult
Or raucous tears dropped on the feet of God

Canons and celestial
Embroidered around,
Glazed eyes
Racing side to side
Erupts the dubious volcano
On Saturn
Where streams of water (like lava)
Melt on the trenches of jealous sprites

A soul ripped in two
Following numb voices
Back at the end of the tunnel
You stand there…

Nothing
echoes
Embellished
Wind,
Fondling and teasing
Meek curiosity

Wash down is a tyrant
Stabbed not by the cacti
But granules belonging
To the shore of Indonesia
Tickled by vestige pilgrims…

Follow me

Splendor...at an end
(A chance encounter with the nymph)

I thought
That I could walk sullen
Quiet like the black lonesome sparrow,
Tired of looking for the other birds
Undisturbed

Wind chimes blowing in the wind
No one notice except me
I thought without a bothersome nymph
That I could find my way through the day

As some child
Picking up rocks in boredom
And throw them fiercely,
As if they were on the bed of a river

But it wasn't quite so....

So out of nowhere
The phantasm of black flowers
Blossomed from within
Embarrassingly,
Grotesque...

My splendor walk came to an end

And as if,
Chained by my sticking flesh inside
A black nymphs head
Knocking like a hostile thud,
Came from out of my chest

A dwarf
Or melancholic wizard
Came from within

His wings which burned holes
Burned
As if scorched
Flew out of my chest
Like a premature butterfly,
Out of its cocoon

He flew up!
Up in the air
As if he had a message
He could carry to the gods!

Joshua Victor

Friedrich...will you paint me

My wish is to stand boldly
Like a gentle lion,
Whose mane blows in the air
Embellishing the majesty of the king

Stare off
Daringly
Like Friedrichs wanderer

Not to think
But feel…
Feel the air

Let me sing
(my journal of bohemia)

There I was by a river
My desire was to see my reflection
And stare at blue and grey burping ripples
Perched up against a trunk
Where bugs make an assembly line,
Climbing up slowly
Whose summer food weighed down their backs
And to see the fluorescent plants sprout like resurrected,
Green nymphs, whose only desire is to cultivate
Red, green, yellow and purple buds

Where solemn bees
Steal their nectar
And fondle weary pedals
Supporting their body whose heavy wings
Make them tired

And
Chestnut brown squirrels run
Hesitantly stopping and going
Simultaneously

Perched up,
On their two feet

Staring at me to see who I am
They say

Joshua Victor

"Why is this human still?
And benign, does his quietness
Scream benevolence
Has this human did some crime,
Out of a grudge
Which was too bad to stay around his inhabitants?
So he came out here to look at us cleverly play,
And find fun looking at us,
As if we're running through a self-built maze
Frolicking
Hysterically laughing,
As we search for food with jubilee

-well maybe squirrel

Oh how the moor encircles this river,
Who sparkles like a lost jewel in the caves,
Of Africa or Egypt

Like the green earth
With a blue luminous hole,
Whose only job is to draw in,
And dress up with alluring setting
Who calls for wanderers, muses, and
Escapers

Oh is the azure
Whose mystic colors
Have been painted by,
The sun setting and sleeping in the clouds
Vomiting,
A smoke of yellow, pink, orange, and scattered colors

My only response is to stare and see
How long will it last
And the dusk coming slowly,
The day envying me or at least,
Tired of me absorbing its bohemian powers...

So it dumps me
Back on the road
Walking with my soul,
Head low
To brown roads
Kicking dust
And
A white bag
Thrown over my shoulder

-Journey through these abysses dear reader

J. Victor

Printed in the United States
By Bookmasters